Contents

Module 1 1
Module 2 7
Module 3 18
Module 4 27
Module 5 34
Module 6 40
Module 7 47
Module 8 54
Module 9 59
Module 10 64
Module 11 70
Module 12 76
Module 13 83
Module 14 88
Module 15 95
Module 16 101
Module 17 107
Module 18 114
Sight Words 124

© 2020 by Accelerate Education
Visit us on the Web at: www.accelerate.education

 My name is _____ .

Read each line of words.
Circle: *is a sentence* or *not a sentence*

Remember that a sentence...
- Has a "who" in it.
- Has a "what happened" in it.
- Begins with a capital.
- Ends with a period.

1. The train up the hill.   is a sentence   not a sentence

2. He can play ball very well.   is a sentence   not a sentence

3. The ball bounced on the ground.   is a sentence   not a sentence

4. Into the house ran.   is a sentence   not a sentence

5. Meg will draw a picture.   is a sentence   not a sentence

6. The cab in front of the building. is a sentence   not a sentence

7. They will ride the bus.   is a sentence   not a sentence

8. The hot handle on the stove.   is a sentence   not a sentence

9. The food is hot.   is a sentence   not a sentence

10. In the window under the stair.   is a sentence   not a sentence

1.1 - Your Family

My name is _____ .

Is it the Same or Different?

The Swing family has a dog but your family may have a cat.

What similarities and differences do you have with the Swing family? Write them down in the chart below.

Similarities	Differences
_____	_____
_____	_____
_____	_____
_____	_____
_____	_____
_____	_____
_____	_____

1.1 - Your Family

My name is _____ .

Reading Comprehension

Answer the questions in complete sentences.

Submit to your teacher.

1) Who is in Meg's family?

2) What does Meg like to do in the morning?

3) Why is Ben grumpy in the morning?

1.2 - Your Family

4) What cheered Ben up?

5) What did Ben and Meg do in their main lesson books?

My name is _____.

- Read each line of words.
- Decide if it is a sentence or not a sentence.
- Decide why it is or is not a sentence.
- Then circle your answer.

1. The bird can fly.   (is a sentence)   not a sentence

2. Into the store.   is a sentence   (not a sentence)

3. Sarah under a tree.   is a sentence   (not a sentence)

4. The bat hit the ball.   (is a sentence)   not a sentence

5. The paper fell on the floor.   (is a sentence)   not a sentence

6. On the ground fell.   is a sentence   (not a sentence)

7. Over the bridge and to the store.   is a sentence   (not a sentence)

8. The car can go fast.   (is a sentence)   not a sentence

5   1.2 - Your Family

Name _____.

Spelling Test

Directions: As your teacher reads your words, write each spelling word on the blanks below.

1) _____

2) _____

3) _____

4) _____

5) _____

6) _____

7) _____

8) _____

9) _____

10) _____

1.5 - Your Family

 **Family Vacation**

2.2.1 Grammar Worksheet

Name _____ .

Sentence Subject

Directions: Circle the subject of each sentence. The subject is the is the "who" or "what" that does something in the sentence.

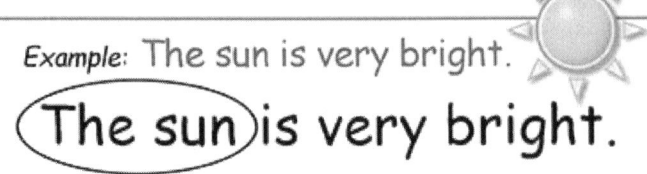
Example: The sun is very bright.
(The sun) is very bright.

1) The table is long.

2) He sat on the table.

3) The red ball bounced up and down.

4) Pat bounced the green ball up and down.

5) A book fell on the floor.

6) The bird sat in the tree.

7) The cat ran after the bird.

8) The big dog ate the bone.

9) The bright star moved in the sky.

7

2.1 - Family Fun

Family Vacation

2.1 Writing Brainstorm

Name _____

Writing Brainstorm

List the things that you like to do when you are having fun with your family members. Write informational paragraphs about what you like to do for fun with your family.

1. _____

_____

_____

_____

_____

2. _____

_____

_____

_____

_____

2.1 - Family Fun   8

3.

4.

5.

2.1 - Family Fun

My name is _____.

Reading Comprehension

Answer the questions in complete sentences.

1) What did Ben and Meg do with the clothes in the box, a table, and a blanket?

2) Why didn't Ben want Chip in the playhouse? How do you know?

3) Where do you think Dad was? Why did he come home?

Continue on next page.

2.2 - Family Fun

4) After lunch, what did Ben and Meg do first with their Mother? What did they do second?

5) What did Ben and Meg do with the acorns they gathered?

2.2 - Family Fun

2.4 Grammar Worksheet

_____.

ntence with a subject

climbed the tree.

Family Vacation

2.2 Writing First Draft

Writing First Draft

Name _____.

Write a first draft paragraph about one or two things that you do to have fun with your family.

Take a look at the list of things that you like to do for fun with your family. Choose one or two things that you want to write more about.

When you write more, you write details. Details provide more information.

Example: Thomas likes to play checkers with his family on Friday nights.

His paragraph will include details about playing checkers.

Details may include: **Details**

1. A special name for game night
2. How to play checkers
3. Why checkers is fun

Write your first draft. Then submit it to your teacher.

_____
_____
_____
_____
_____
_____
_____
_____
_____
_____

Continue on following page

Family Vacation

Name _____

Writing Sentences

Write a sentence. Use the word below in the s

1) leg

2.2 - Family Fun

Name _____.

Spelling Test

Directions: As your teacher reads your words, write each spelling word on the blanks below.

1) _____

2) _____

3) _____

4) _____

5) _____

6) _____

7) _____

8) _____

9) _____

10) _____

2.5 - Family Fun

Family Vacation

2.5 Family Fun Paragraph

Name _____.

Publish

You have your brainstorm, first draft, revision, and edit papers. See how your paragraph has changed. Write your paragraph in your best handwriting and draw a picture to illustrate it. Share it. Now you have published.

Grammar Sentences

My name is _____.

Predicates

Circle the **predicate** of each sentence.

The predicate is what the subject "is doing" or "is" in a sentence. It can be more than one word.

1. She listens to her mother.

2. The bird sat on the branch.

3. You should walk down the stairs.

4. The ball rolls.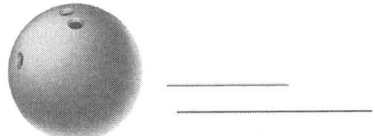

5. A book is closed.

6. The house was built on a hill.

7. The breakfast is cold.

Continue on following page.

3.1 - Bedtime   18

8. Her pretty dress has jelly on it.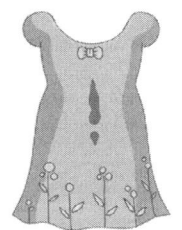

9. The star twinkled in the sky.

10. The dog rolled on his back.

Writing Brainstorm

Name _____ .

List the things that you do before you go to bed each night.

You are going to write an informational paragraph about your bedroom routine.

First **1** ----

Second **2** ----

Third **3** ----

Fourth **4** ----

Fifth **5** ----

3.1 - Bedtime

My name is _____.

Reading Comprehension

Answer the questions in complete sentences.

1) At bedtime, what does Ben do while Meg is taking a bath?

2) Why is it important for Ben to cover the holes on his recorder?

3) Why does Chip bark when Ben plays the recorder?

Continue on the next page.

4) What does Daddy do after playing the recorder with Ben?

5) What do Ben and Meg do right before they go to sleep?

2.4 Grammar Worksheet

Name _____.

Missing Predicate

Directions: Complete the sentence with one or more words so the predicate makes sense.

1. The clown _____ a wig.

2. The bear _____ at the park visitors.

3. The giant bird _____.

4. The egg _____ when it _____.

5. The children _____.

23 3.4 - Bedtime

Name _____.

Spelling Test

Directions: As your teacher reads your words, write each spelling word on the blanks below.

1) _____

2) _____

3) _____

4) _____

5) _____

6) _____

7) _____

8) _____

9) _____

10) _____

3.5 - Bedtime

3.5 Grammar Worksheet

My name is _____.

Writing Sentences

Directions: Write a sentence that contains both words.

squeak, house

lively, cat

trouble, school

Continue on the following page.

3.5 - Bedtime

thought, listened

each, beautiful

Neighborhoods

My name is _____.

Does the sentence **ask** or **tell**? Punctuate each sentence with a period or question mark.

1. Will you eat eggs for breakfast ☐

2. The corn stalks are very tall ☐

3. Apples come in different colors ☐

4. Do you like to drink apple juice or orange juice ☐

5. The leaf pile is tall ☐

6. How do you feel about playing tag ☐

7. Can you walk to the corner with me ☐

8. I have little time to work ☐

9. Could you help me wrap this ☐

10. Who can jump the highest ☐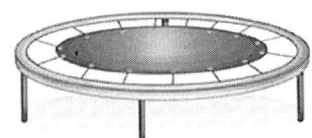

27   4.1 - Fall Fun

Neighborhoods

Name _____

Writing Brainstorm

What do you know about the fall season? What is the weather like? What do people do outside? What foods do you eat?

Make a list of three or four things that you like to do during the fall season.

 1	
 2	
 3	
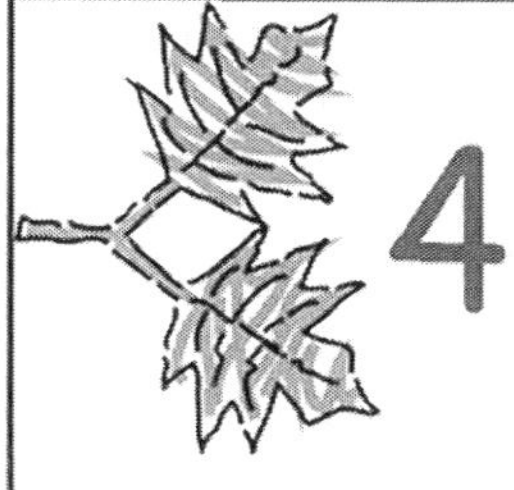 4	

4.1 - Fall Fun

My name is _____.

Reading Comprehension

Answer the questions in complete sentences.

1) Close your eyes and picture Vermont in the fall. Describe what you see?

_____
_____
_____
_____

2) Why do you think Ben and Meg did not pay attention when they first smelled the smoke?

_____
_____
_____
_____

3) Why was it an "exciting" afternoon?

_____
_____
_____
_____

Continue on next page.

29   4.2 - Fall Fun

4) Why does the big truck deliver wood every fall?

5) Why is the middle of October a good time to visit Vermont?

4.2 - Fall Fun

My name is _____ .

Question or Statement

Complete the sentence with one or more words so the sentence makes sense.

1. _____ did the clown look sad?

2. _____ played with her cat.

3. _____ you eat breakfast?

4. _____ many eggs are in the carton?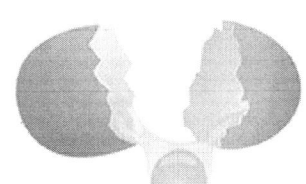

5. _____ to the store with me.

31   4.4 - Fall Fun

Name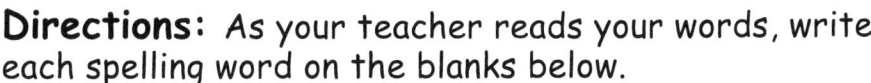

Spelling Test

Directions: As your teacher reads your words, write each spelling word on the blanks below.

1) _____

2) _____

3) _____

4) _____

5) _____

6) _____

7) _____

8) _____

9) _____

10) _____

4.5 - Fall Fun

My name is _____.

Sentences

Write a sentence that contains both words in the boxes below.

mountains, snow
brightest, children
know, leaves
chlorophyll, green
chemicals, change

4.5 - Fall Fun

5.1 Grammar Worksheet

Name _____

Nouns

Directions: Circle the (common nouns) and underline the proper nouns in each sentence.

1. I like to eat cereal for breakfast.

2. His name is Jared Henley.

3. I like red apples that you can pick in Lancaster, PA.

4. The water in the bathtub is too high.

5. I went to the office after I got in trouble.

6. The best oranges are from Florida.

7. The grocery store in Centreville is bigger.

8. Mrs. Bell is our troop leader.

9. The tallest monument is in Washington, D.C.

10. The dog did not want to play ball.

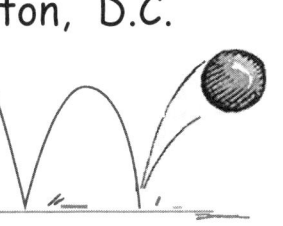

5.1 Writing Brainstorm

Name _____

Writing Brainstorm

Do you know how to change a light bulb? Brainstorm some things that you can do well.

Make a list of three or four things that you do well.

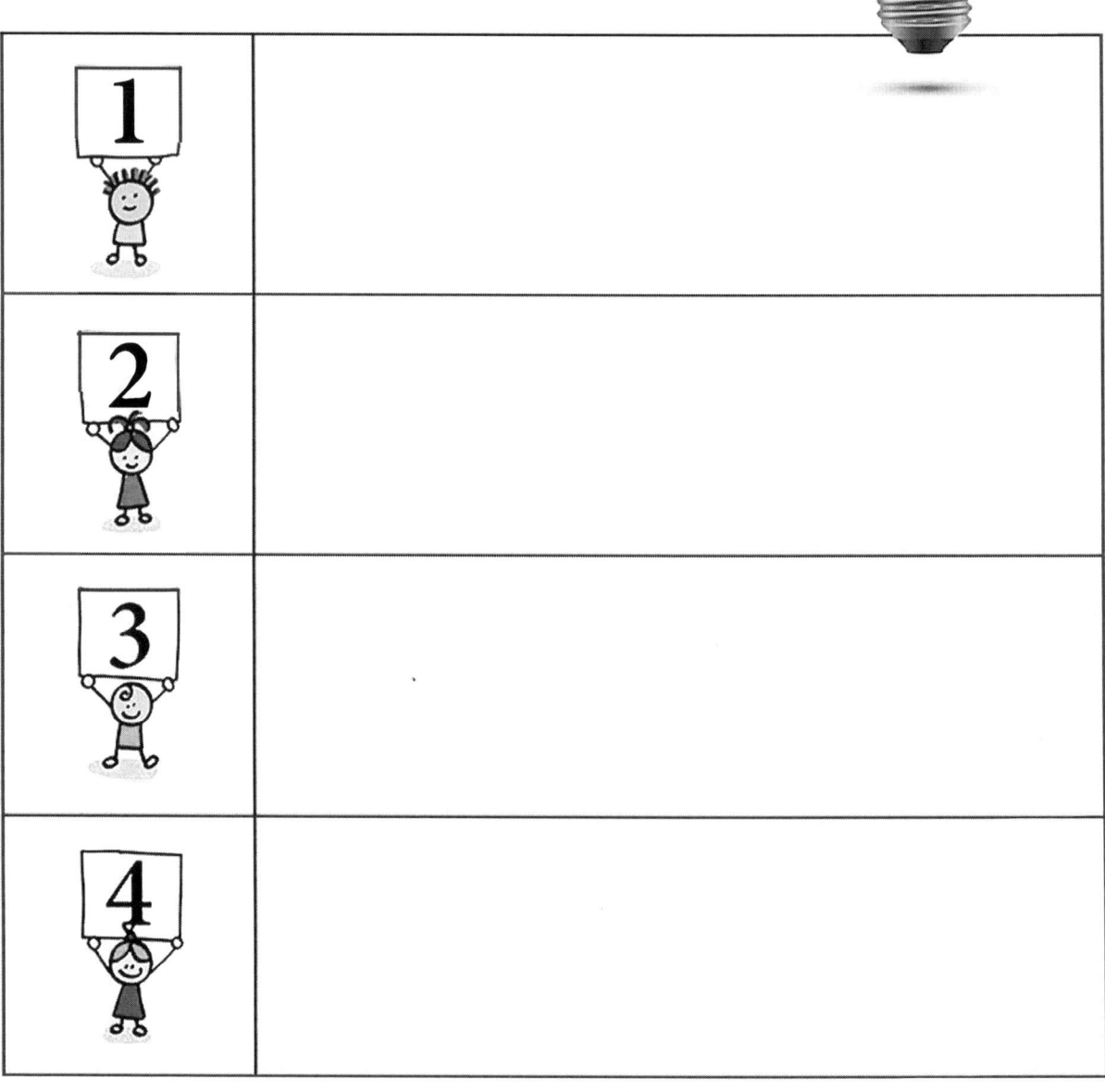

35   5.1 - Farm Visit

My name is _____.

Writing Sentences

Write a sentence that contains the sight word in the boxes below.

old

round

them

when

again

5.2 - Farm Visit

My name is _____.

Reading Comprehension

Directions: Answer the questions below in complete sentences.

1) What were Ben, Meg, and Mother going to make when they returned from the farm?

2) How did Ben, Meg, and Mother get the big pumpkin to the car?

3) How did Ben, Meg, and Mother get the pumpkin out of the car?

Continue on next page.

5.2 - Farm Visit

4) What did Ben, Meg, and Mother do with the big pumpkin?

5) Where did Ben, Meg, and Mother plan to go next?

5.2 - Farm Visit

Name _____.

Spelling Test

Directions: As your teacher reads your words, write each spelling word on the blanks below.

1) _____

2) _____

3) _____

4) _____

5) _____

6) _____

7) _____

8) _____

9) _____

10) _____

My name is _____ .

Writing Brainstorm

What do you think you would have to do to become a dentist, firefighter, teacher, or something else?
What do you think they do?
Pick one and write your answers below.

6.1 - Dentist Visit

40

My name is _____ .

Writing Sentences

Write a sentence that contains the sight word in the boxes below.

then
an
could
going
his

6.2 - Dentist Visit

My name is _____.

Reading Comprehension

Answer the questions in complete sentences.

Submit to your teacher.

1) What does Meg like to do at the Dentist's office?

2) Why is it important to get your teeth cleaned at the dentist's office?

3) What was Meg's good news when she got out of the dentist's chair?

6.2 - Dentist Visit

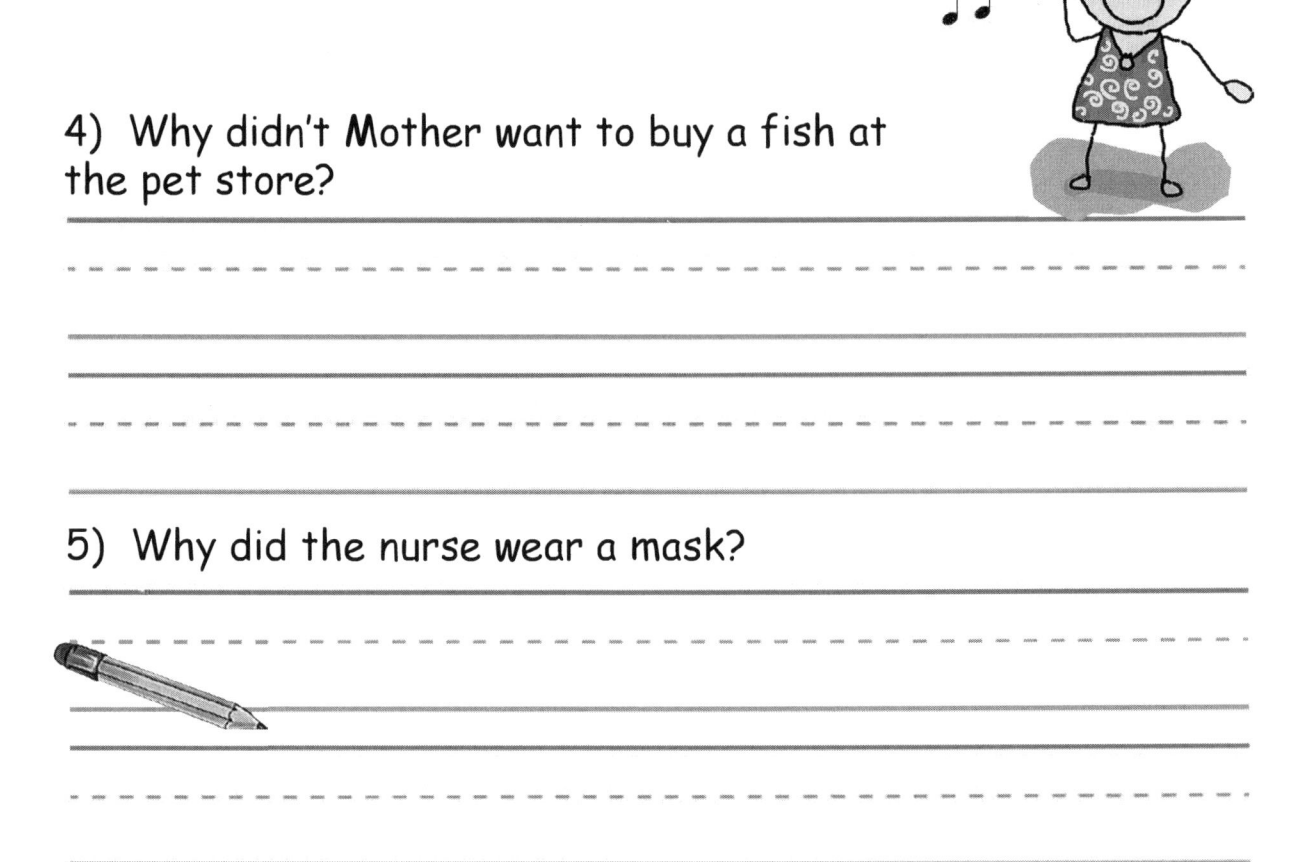

4) Why didn't Mother want to buy a fish at the pet store?

5) Why did the nurse wear a mask?

My name is _____.

Singular or Plural

Directions: Correct the noun in each sentence.
If the sentence is correct, put a "C" in the box.

1. ☐ The one big boxes will not fit in the car. _____

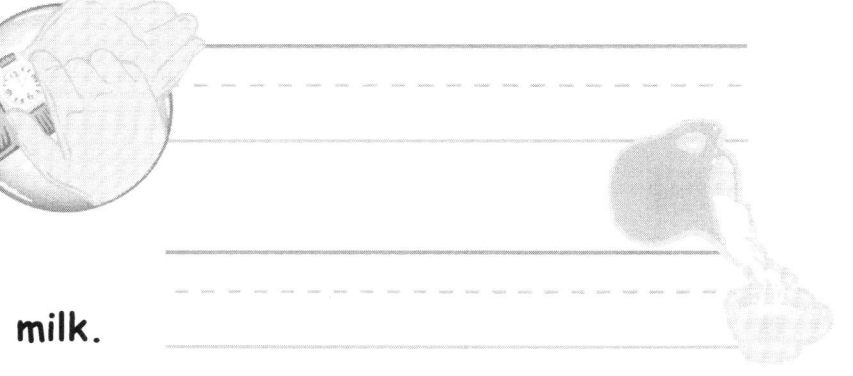

2. ☐ I wear one watch on my wrist. _____

3. ☐ Go to the store to get two can of milk. _____

4. ☐ I won two game of checkers on the way to grandmother's house. _____

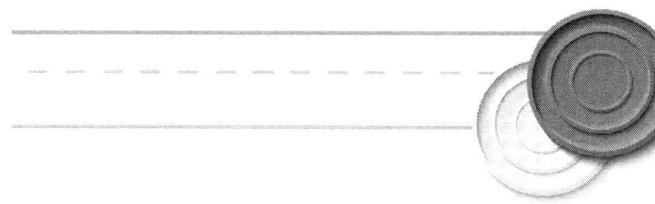

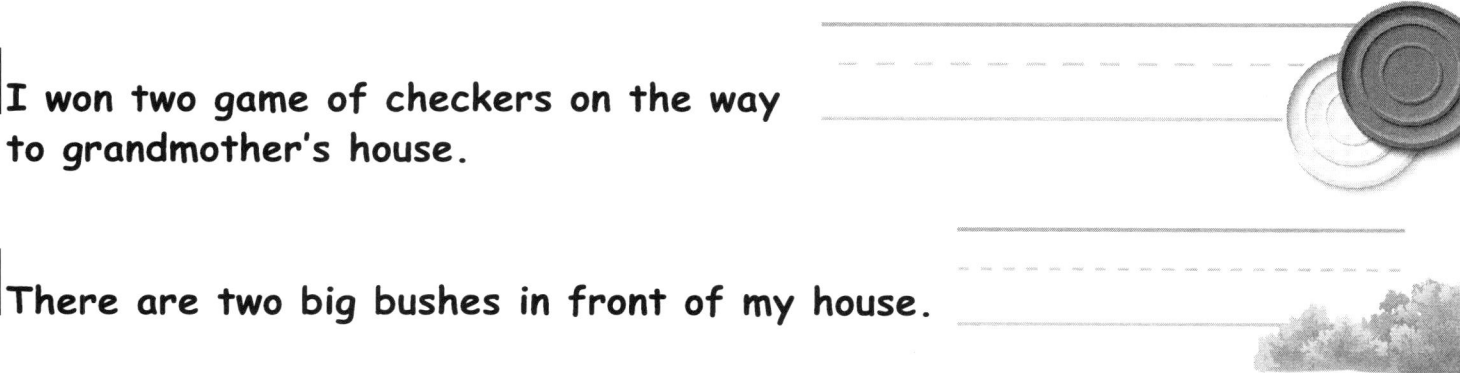

5. ☐ There are two big bushes in front of my house. _____

6.4 - Dentist Visit

Name _____.

Spelling Test

Directions: As your teacher reads your words, write each spelling word on the blanks below.

1) _____

2) _____

3) _____

4) _____

5) _____

6) _____

7) _____

8) _____

9) _____

10) _____

My name is _____.

Writing Sentences

Write a sentence that contains both words.

_____

climbed, higher

people, have

Dr., office

already, go

flu, sick

6.5 - Dentist Visit

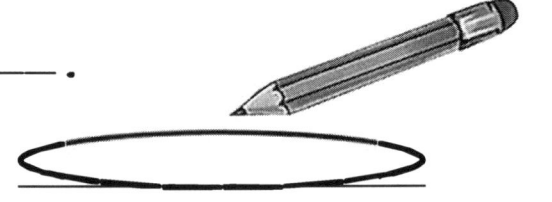

7.1 Grammar Sentences

My name is _____.

Grammar - *Grandparents*

Circle the collective noun in the sentence.
(**Collective nouns** name a group of things.)

1. Eat your stack of pancakes.

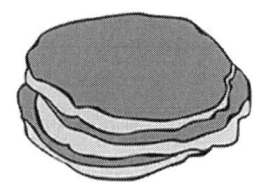

2. Let's play "Old Maid" with the deck of cards.

3. You can see a lion pride from the jeep.

4. Don't run from the swarm of bees.

5. The flower bunch smells good.

6. That group of students can walk to the bus.

7.1 Writing Brainstorm

Name _____.

Writing - *Grandparents*

Do you have a fun story to share about a time with your grandparents? Brainstorm some things that you've done with your grandparents.

Make a list of three or four things below that you and your grandparents have done together.

1	
2	
3	
4	

7.1 - Grandparents

7.2 Reading Comprehension

My name is _____.

Reading - *Grandparents*

Directions: Answer the questions below in complete sentences.

1) Why do Ben and Meg like visiting their Grandmother?

_____

_____

_____

_____

2) What does Meg like to do at her grandmother's?

_____

_____

_____

3) Why did Ben get the wood?

_____

_____

_____

_____

Continue on the following page.

4) What type of pie do Ben and Meg like to eat?

5) What did Ben decide to write about when he got home?

7.4 Writing Sentences

My name is _____.

Sentences - *Grandparents*

Write a sentence that contains the **collective noun** in the boxes below.

pride
bunch
stack
swarm
school

Name _____.

Spelling Test

Directions: As your teacher reads your words, write each spelling word on the blanks below.

1) _____

2) _____

3) _____

4) _____

5) _____

6) _____

7) _____

8) _____

9) _____

10) _____

My name is _____.

Sentences - *Grandparents*

Write a sentence that contains both words in the boxes below.

vegetable, decided
wondered, carrying
crocheting, knitting
right, cruel
better, tapping

8.1 Writing Brainstorm

Name _____

"Snow" Story - *Making Snow*

Brainstorm the elements for a story you will write about snow.

Characters

Setting

Character Action

Character Action

Ending

8.1 - Making Snow 54

My name is _____.

Reading Comprehension - *Making Snow*

Answer the questions in complete sentences.

1) What did Ben and Meg have to do before they could go sledding?

2) What did Ben and Meg do until it stopped snowing?

3) Why did Daddy shovel snow off the roof?

4) What did Ben and Meg do the morning after the first snowfall?

Continue on the next page.

5) What did Ben and Meg use to make the snow look like a man?

6) What did Chip do to have fun?

7) What did Ben and Meg learn about at the library?

8) What animals made the tracks in the snow?

Name _____ .

Spelling Test

Directions: As your teacher reads your words, write each spelling word on the blanks below.

1) _____

2) _____

3) _____

4) _____

5) _____

6) _____

7) _____

8) _____

9) _____

10) _____

My name is _____.

Sentences - *Making Snow*

Write a sentence that contains both words in the boxes below.

guess, couldn't
eyes, through
cocoa, enough
weight, science
magnifying, towards

8.5 - Making Snow

9.1 Writing Brainstorm

My name is _____.

Poetry - *Winter Time*

Brainstorm ideas about a poem that you can write about **winter**. You can draw pictures or just write a few key words to help you remember your ideas.

My poem can be about...

Idea 1:

Idea 2:

Idea 3:

Idea 4:

Idea 5:

9.1 - Winter Fun

9.2 Reading Comprehension

My name is _____.

Reading - *Winter Time*

Answer the questions below about the story, "**Winter Fun**".

1) Who learned to ice skate for the first time?

2) What do ice fishermen do to get to the water?

3) What new things did Ben learn to do on the ice when skating?

4) How long did Ben and Meg skate before they got cold?

Continue on the next page.

9.2 - Winter Fun

5) How do ice fishermen keep warm?

6) What did Ben and Meg learn to do at the outdoor education center?

Name_____

Spelling Test

Directions: As your teacher reads your words, write each spelling word on the blanks below.

1) _____

2) _____

3) _____

4) _____

5) _____

6) _____

7) _____

8) _____

9) _____

9.5 Writing Sentences

My name is _____.

Sentences - *Winter Time*

Write a sentence that contains both words in the boxes below.

always, best
does, read
found, us
made, your
tell, why

9.5 - Winter Fun

10.1 Writing Brainstorm

My name is _____.

Writing - Cooking Fun

Explain why you like your favorite foods? Write your answers in the boxes below.

I like... because...

I like... because...

I like... because...

I like... because...

I like... because...

10.1 - Cooking Fun

10.2 Reading Comprehension

My name is _____.

Reading - *Cooking Fun*

Directions: Answer the questions below about "**Maple Syrup**".

1) Why did Mother want Ben to be careful with the maple syrup?

2) What does it mean to tap a tree?

3) Where was Chip?

Continue on the following page.

4) Why did Mother say that they would have to go outside when Chip was let out?

5) What is maple syrup?

10.2 - Cooking Fun

Name _____.

Spelling Test

Directions: As your teacher reads your words, write each spelling word on the blanks below.

1) _____

2) _____

3) _____

4) _____

5) _____

6) _____

7) _____

8) _____

9) _____

10.5 - Cooking Fun

My name is _____.

Sentences - *Cooking Fun*

Write a sentence that contains both words in the boxes below.

around, their

| both, gave |
| |

| don't, paint |
| |

| use, many |
| |

| with, hand |
| |

Name _____

Story Map - *Cooking Fun*

10.5 Reading Worksheet

Maple Syrup

Directions: Complete the story map to identify the main characters, setting, and events in the story, "**Maple Syrup**". Explain any problems and solutions.

Story Map

The Characters:
(Who)

Title:
Maple Syrup

The Setting:
(Where)

Events:
(What)

Event 1:

Event 2:

Event 3:

Problem:

Solution:

69

10.5 - Cooking Fun

Name _____

11.1 Writing Brainstorm

Writing - *Cycles*

Draw a picture of the life cycle of a butterfly (caterpillar to butterfly) below.

11.1 - Cycles

11.2 Reading Comprehension

My name is _____.

Reading - Cycles

Answer the questions below about the story, "**Tadpoles**".

1) During what season are the frogs still eggs?

_____
_____
_____

2) How are the eggs protected?

_____
_____
_____

3) What animals eat many of the frog eggs?

_____
_____
_____

4) What happened when Meg leaned over the pond?

_____
_____
_____

Continue on the next page.

5) Why didn't Mother want Ben and Meg to take the tadpoles out of the pond?

6) What makes drawing easier for Ben?

Name _____.

Spelling Test

Directions: As your teacher reads your words, write each spelling word on the blanks below.

1) _____

2) _____

3) _____

4) _____

5) _____

6) _____

7) _____

8) _____

9) _____

10) _____

My name is _____

Sentences - *Cycles*

Write a sentence that contains both words in the boxes below.

11.5 Writing Sentences

because, easier

goes, distance

sing, rock

kick, very

work, fast

11.5 - Cycles

Name _____

Story Map - *Cycles*

Directions: Complete the story map to identify the main characters, setting, and events in the story, "**Tadpoles**". Explain any problems and solutions.

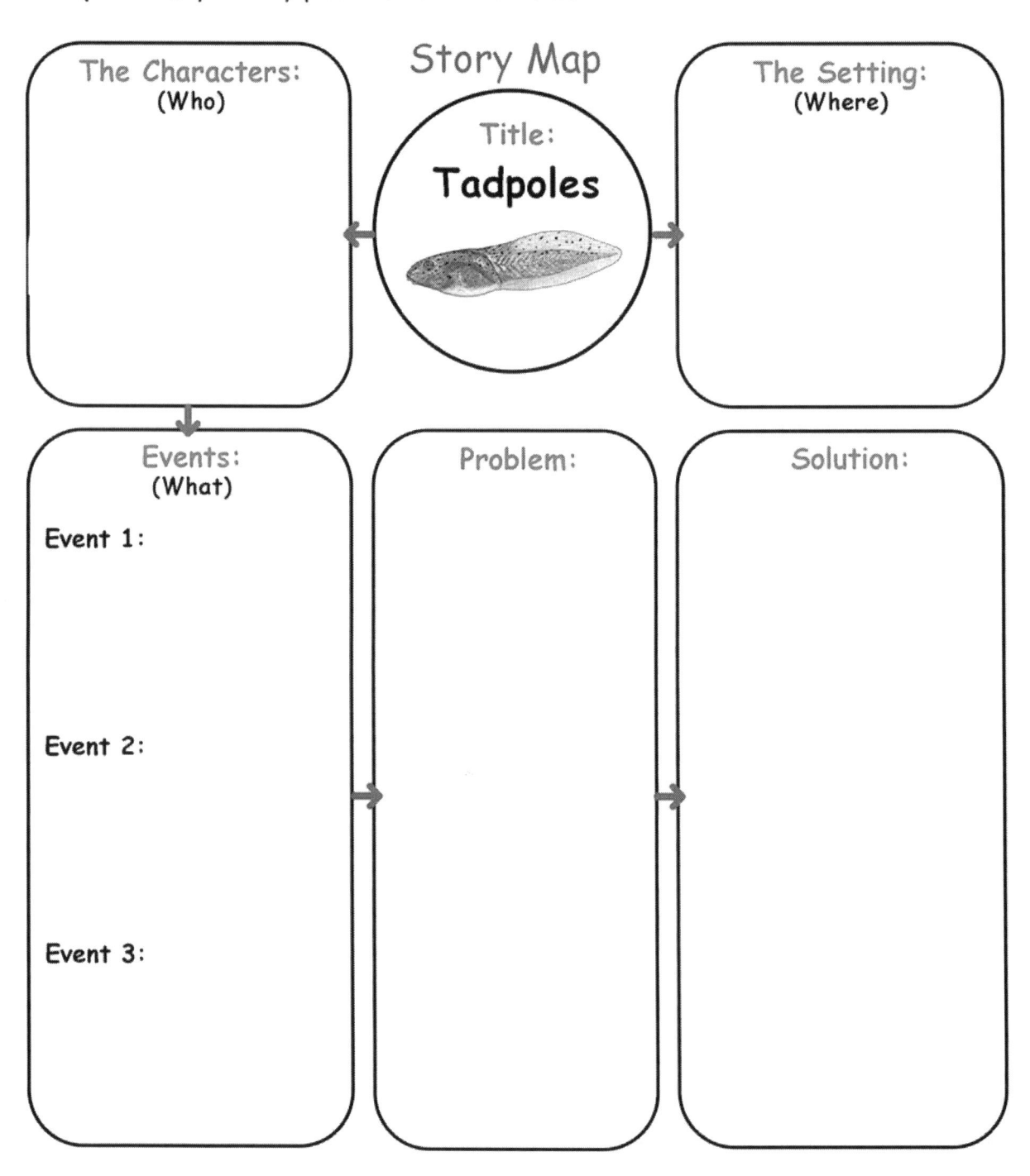

11.5 Reading Worksheet

Tadpoles

Story Map

Title: **Tadpoles**

The Characters:
(Who)

The Setting:
(Where)

Events:
(What)

Event 1:

Event 2:

Event 3:

Problem:

Solution:

75

11.5 - Cycles

12.1 Writing Brainstorm

My name is _____ .

Facts and Opinions - *Getting Creative*

Write three facts about what you **see** and three opinions about what you **think** about the painting. Write your facts and opinions on the following page.

Continue on the next page.

12.1 - Getting Creative								76

List what do you see in the painting (**facts**) and what do you think about the painting (**opinions**) below.

Facts	Opinions

12.2 Reading Comprehension

My name is _____.

Reading - *Getting Creative*

Answer the questions below about the story, "**Afternoon Treat**".

1) What kind of pot did Ben and Meg make?

2) What did Chip do with the pot?

3) Where did Mother, Ben, and Meg go after lunch?

4) Why do you think the bird did not eat Meg's cookie?

Continue on the next page.

12.2 - Getting Creative

5) What is a General Store?

6) Why couldn't Ben and Meg visit the school?

Name _____.

Spelling Test

Directions: As your teacher reads your words, write each spelling word on the blanks below.

1) _____

2) _____

3) _____

4) _____

5) _____

6) _____

7) _____

8) _____

9) _____

10) _____

12.5 - Getting Creative

12.5 Writing Sentences

My name is _____.

Sentences - *Getting Creative*

Write a sentence that contains both words in the boxes below.

groceries, wallet

might, crowded

sign, video

choose, laugh

least, years

81   12.5 - Getting Creative

Name _____

12.5 Reading Worksheet

Afternoon Treat

Story Map - *Getting Creative*

Directions: Complete the story map to identify the main characters, setting, and events in the story, "**Afternoon Treat**". Explain any problems and solutions.

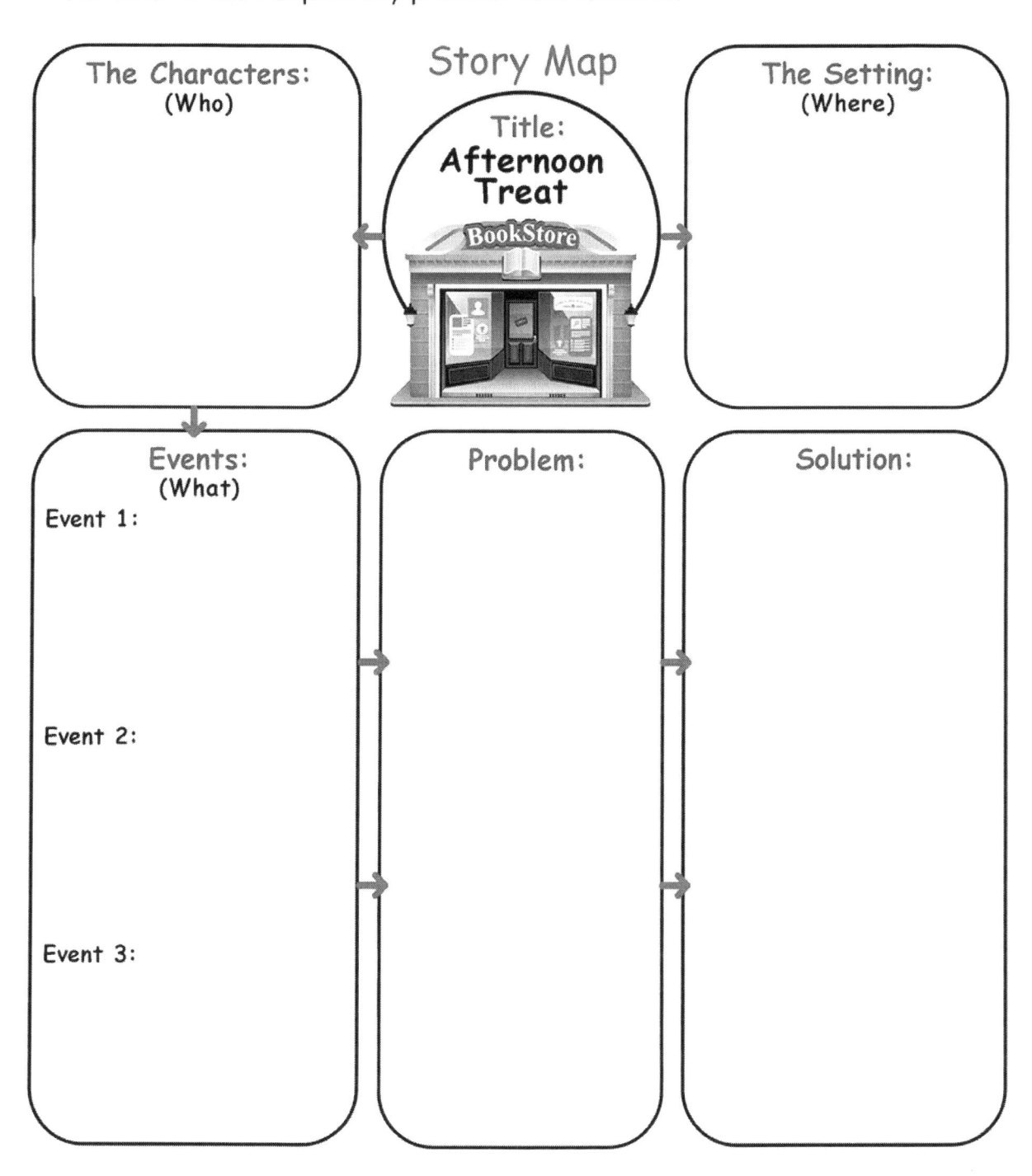

Story Map

Title: Afternoon Treat

The Characters: (Who)

The Setting: (Where)

Events: (What)
- Event 1:
- Event 2:
- Event 3:

Problem:

Solution:

12.5 - Getting Creative

13.1 Writing Brainstorm

My name is _____.

Ben and Meg Review -
Fun with Friends

Write about the adventures of Ben and Meg. List where they went and what they did below.

Where did they go?	What did they do?

13.2 Reading Comprehension

My name is _____ .

Reading - *Fun with Friends*

Answer the questions below about the story, "**Sharing**".

1) What are some of the "**same things**" that you, Ben and Meg like to do?

2) Describe where you live. How is it the same or different from where Ben and Meg live?

3) If you visited Vermont, where would you like to go and why?

Name _____.

Spelling Test

Directions: As your teacher reads your words, write each spelling word on the blanks below.

1) _____

2) _____

3) _____

4) _____

5) _____

6) _____

7) _____

8) _____

9) _____

Name _____

Story Map - *Fun with Friends*

13.5 Reading Worksheet

The Talkative Tortoise

Directions: Complete the story map to identify the main characters, setting, and events in the story, "The Talkative Tortoise". Explain any problems and solutions.

Story Map

The Characters:
(Who)

Title: The Talkative Tortoise

The Setting:
(Where)

Events:
(What)

Event 1:

Event 2:

Event 3:

Problem:

Solution:

13.5 - Fun with Friends

86

13.5 Writing Sentences

My name is _____.

Sentences - *Fun with Friends*

Write a sentence in the present tense using the singular or plural form of the verb indicated in parentheses ( ).

fly (singular)

wash (singular)

pay (plural)

go (plural)

fix (singular)

14.1 Grammar Worksheet

My name is _____.

Punctuation- *Animal Friends*

Directions:
Read the passage from "**The Family**" below. Put **quotation marks** and **commas** where they belong.

Don't cry, little kittens said Lizzie. You are going to meet your new families. You will like your new homes.

14.1 Writing Brainstorm

My name is _____ .

Dialogue - *Animal Friends*

Who have you talked to over the past week? What did you talk about? Write the details in the boxes below.

Details

Details

Details

89

14.1 - Animal Friends

14.2 Reading Comprehension

My name is _____.

Reading - *Animal Friends*

Answer the questions below about the story "**The Family**."

1) What are Franky, Pippi, and Bobby?

2) Why did the kittens have to leave Lizzie's house?

3) How did the kittens get out of the basket?

4) What did Ezra and Lizzie use to help get the kittens back into the basket?

Continue on the next page.

14.2 - Animal Friends

5) Who did the two lost kittens belong to?

6) How did Pippi get her name?

Name _____ .

Spelling Test

Directions: As your teacher reads your words, write each spelling word on the blanks below.

1) _____

2) _____

3) _____

4) _____

5) _____

6) _____

7) _____

8) _____

9) _____

10) _____

14.5 - Animal Friends

Name _____

14.5 Reading Worksheet

Story Map - *Animal Friends*

The Family

Directions: Complete the story map to identify the main characters, setting and events in the story, "The Family". Explain any problems and solutions.

Story Map

The Characters:
(Who)

Title:
The Family

The Setting:
(Where)

Events:
(What)

Event 1:

Event 2:

Event 3:

Problem:

Solution:

93

14.5 - Animal Friends

14.5 Grammar Worksheet

My name is _____.

Punctuate the Dialogue -
Animal Friends

Directions:
Read the passage from **"The Gingerbread Man"** below. Add **quotation marks** and **commas** where needed.

The fox began to run faster, and the little Gingerbread Boy ran faster, and as he ran he chuckled and said I have run away from a little old woman, a little old man, a cow, a horse, a barn full of threshers, and a field full of mowers, and I can run away from you, I can, I can!

Run, run, run, as fast as you can! You can't catch me, I'm the Gingerbread Man!

Why, said the fox I would not catch you if I could. I would not think of disturbing you.

Just then, the little Gingerbread Boy came to a river. He could not swim across, and he wanted to keep running away from the cow and the horse and the people.

Jump on my tail, and I will take you across the river said the fox.

14.5 - Animal Friends

15.1 Writing Brainstorm

My name is _____ .

Picnic Plans - *Animal Helpers*

Lets plan a picnic! You may need to use a search engine to find ideas and list them below. Have an adult watch you.

Possible places to go:

Possible foods to eat:

Possible games to play:

15.2 Reading Comprehension

My name is _____.

Reading - *Animal Helpers*

Directions: Answer the questions below about the story, "**Bobby's Stinky Adventure**".

1) Why is Bobby stiff?

2) What did Bobby do on the ride to the picnic?

3) What is the first thing that the Carters did when they got to the park?

4) How did Bobby come upon a skunk?

Continue on the next page.

15.2 - Animal Helpers

5) Why did the skunk spray Bobby?

6) What did the skunk do when Bobby wanted to play?

Name _____.

Spelling Test

Directions: As your teacher reads your words, write each spelling word on the blanks below.

1) _____

2) _____

3) _____

4) _____

5) _____

6) _____

7) _____

8) _____

9) _____

10) _____

Name _____

15.5 Reading Worksheet

Story Map - *Animal Helpers*

Bobby's Stinky Adventure

Directions: Complete the story map to identify the main characters, setting and events in the story, "Bobby's Stinky Adventure". Explain any problems and solutions.

Story Map

The Characters:
(Who)

Title:
Bobby's Stinky Adventure

The Setting:
(Where)

Events:
(What)

Event 1:

Event 2:

Event 3:

Problem:

Solution:

99

15.5 - Animal Helpers

15.5 Grammar Worksheet

My name is _____.

Future Tense - *Animal Helpers*

Directions: Rewrite the sentences below in the future tense.

1. The fox runs fast.

2. I see the skunk out of the corner of my eye.

3. We have peanut butter and jelly for lunch.

Continue on the following page.

16.1 Writing Brainstorm

My name is _____.

Dog's Point of View -
Animal Babies

Write three ideas for your story from a dog's point of view.

Idea 1:

Idea 2:

Idea 3:

101 16.1 - Animal Babies

16.2 Reading Comprehension

My name is _____.

Reading - *Animal Babies*

Directions: Answer the questions below about the story, "**Pixie's New Home**".

1) Why does Mom think that having another dog would be good for Bobby?

_____

_____

2) Where did Pixie live before moving in with the Carters?

_____

_____

3) Why did it take a while for Pixie to get adopted?

_____

_____

4) Why did Pixie have a lot to learn?

_____

_____

Continue on the next page.

16.2 - Animal Babies

5) Why did the Carter's take Pixie home a while before adopting her?

6) How did Bobby react to Pixie?

Name _____.

Spelling Test

Directions: As your teacher reads your words, write each spelling word on the blanks below.

1) _____

2) _____

3) _____

4) _____

5) _____

6) _____

7) _____

8) _____

9) _____

10) _____

Name _____.

16.5 Reading Worksheet

Story Map - *Animal Babies*

Pixie's New Home

Directions: Complete the story map to identify the main characters, setting, and events in the story, "**Pixie's New Home**". Explain any problems and solutions.

Story Map

Title: Pixie's New Home

The Characters: (Who)

The Setting: (Where)

Events: (What)
- Event 1:
- Event 2:
- Event 3:

Problem:

Solution:

105

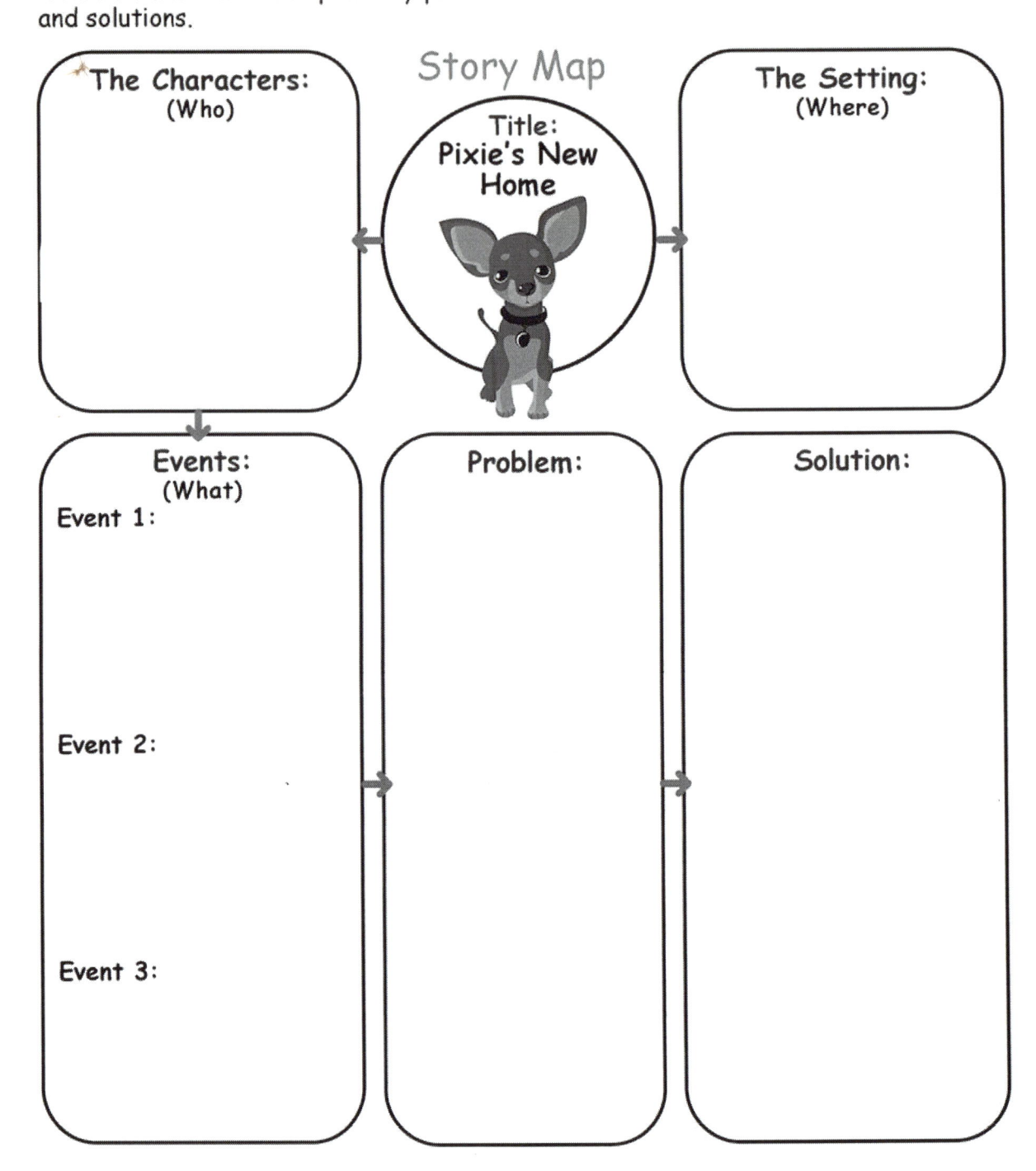

16.5 - Animal Babies

Name: _____

Put the Commas in the Sentence

Place the commas in each sentence to separate the things or things to do in the list. The things or things to do can have more than one word.

Example: We like to swim, play kickball, and eat ice cream at the park.

1.) I have a pet dog cat and parrot.

2.) You can make crafts look at stars and go on hikes at camp.

3.) Mix yellow blue and white to make light green.

4.) If you add the numbers one three four and five it equals 13.

5.) You can jump rope swing or play hopscotch at recess.

16.5 - Animal Babies

My name is _____.

Writing - *Animals Eat*

17.1 Writing Brainstorm

Directions: Choose an animal to research or observe how and what it eats. Write your animal on the line below. Then, brainstorm how and what your animal eats. When you have finished you can observe or research to find more information.

What animal will you observe or research? _____

Brainstorm what and how your animal eats. How is this different from you? Write your animal in the middle circle. Write your brainstorm ideas in the circles around your animal.

107 17.1 - Animals Eat

17.2 Reading Comprehension

My name is _____.

Reading - Animals Eat

Answer the questions below about the story, **"The Crow Has a Snack"**.

1) Where are Franky and Pippi sitting while they watch the crow?

2) What did the crow see that he wanted to eat while he was flying?

3) What did Franky and Pippi want to play with the crow?

4) How did the crow break open the walnut?

Continue on the next page.

17.2 - Animals Eat   108

5) Why did the crow need to drop the walnut to open it?

Name _____.

Spelling Test

Directions: As your teacher reads your words, write each spelling word on the blanks below.

1) _____

2) _____

3) _____

4) _____

5) _____

6) _____

7) _____

8) _____

9) _____

10) _____

Name _____.

Story Map - *Animals Eat*

17.5 Reading Worksheet

The Crow Has a Snack

Directions: Complete the story map to identify the main characters, setting, and events in the story, "**The Crow Has a Snack**". Explain any problems and solutions.

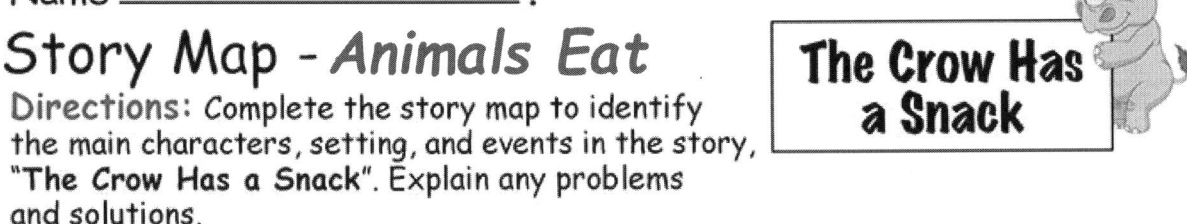

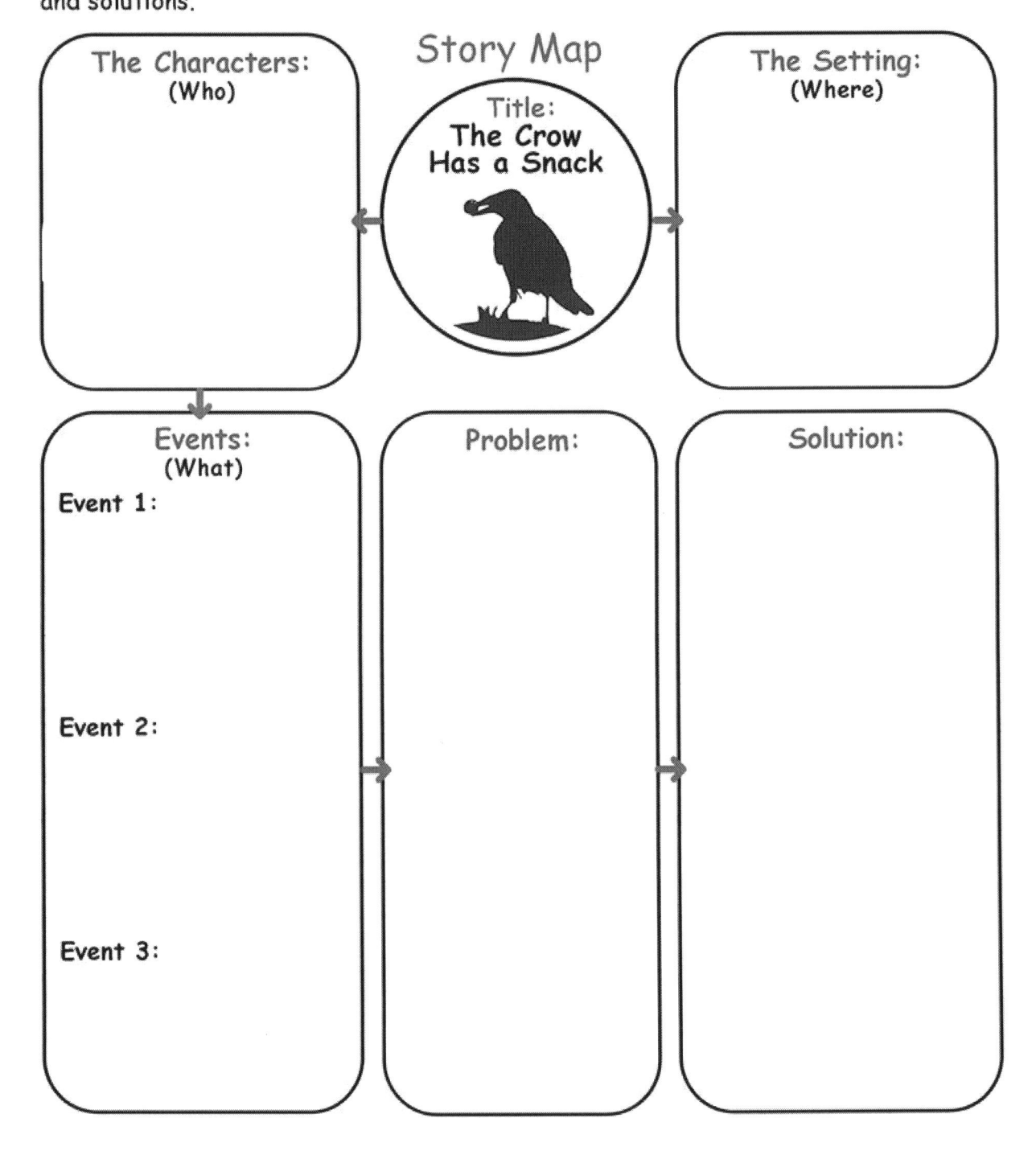

Story Map

The Characters: (Who)

Title: The Crow Has a Snack

The Setting: (Where)

Events: (What)

Event 1:

Event 2:

Event 3:

Problem:

Solution:

17.5 - Animals Eat

17.5 Grammar Worksheet

Name _____.

Singular and Plural Pronouns -
Animals Eat

Directions: Rewrite each sentence below about the story, "The Crow Has a Snack". Replace the **bold** word with a matching singular or plural pronoun.

1. **Walnuts** have a hard shell.

2. The crow gave **Pippi** a "you can't catch me" look.

3. The **crow** dropped the walnuts from up high.

Continue on the next page.

17.5 - Animals Eat   112

4. **The cats and I** were surprised the crow was clever.

5. **Franky** was sitting on the windowsill.

18.2 Reading Comprehension

My name is _____.

Reading - Animals that Dig

Directions: Answer the questions below about the story, "**Pixie's Surprise**".

1) What is Pixie doing that is wrong?
   _____
   _____
   _____

2) Besides Pixie, who else is digging holes in the yard?
   _____
   _____

3) How did Pixie hurt her leg?
   _____
   _____
   _____

4) What did Pixie find in a hole?
   _____
   _____
   _____

Continue on the next page.

18.2 - Animals That Dig

5) How did Pixie hurt her nose?

6) Will Pixie continue to dig holes? Why or Why not?

18.2 Writing Graphic Organizer

Name _____.

Writing - *Animals that Dig*

Directions: Use the topic you chose to complete the boxes below. List the materials in the notebook.

What is your How To topic?

_____

_____

Title: _____

_____

Materials:

Step 1 _____

Step 2 _____

Step 3 _____

Continue on the following page.

18.2 - Animals That Dig

(Write additional steps below if needed.)

Closing Sentence: _____

_____

_____

18.4 Writing Checklist

Name _____

Writing - *Animals that Dig*

Directions: Reread your writing carefully. Put a check in each box under **Author** as you complete each item.

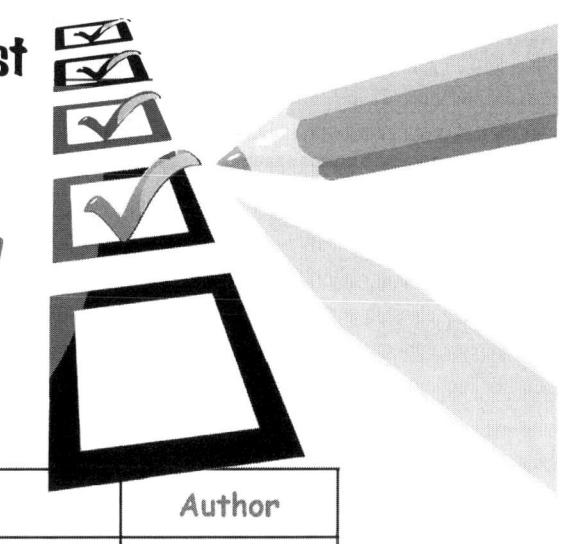

Revise and Edit for the following:	Author
1. Clarity and Meaning **Ask yourself,** "Can the reader complete the topic by following the steps?" "Does the writing piece have a title, steps, and closing sentence?" Rewrite parts that need revision.	

Revise and Edit for the following:	Author
2. Correct Use of Words **Ask yourself,** "Do the sentences sound good together?"" Rewrite parts that need revision.	

Revise and Edit for the following:	Author
3. Capitalization Use capitals at the beginning of each sentence and for every name. Make corrections if needed.	

Continue on the next page.

18.4 - Animals That Dig

Revise and Edit for the following:	Author

4. Punctuation
 	
    Use periods, exclamation points, and question marks.
 	
    Use quotation marks for dialogue.
 	
    Make corrections if needed.	

Revise and Edit for the following:	Author

5. Spelling
 	
    Check for correct spelling.
 	
    Make corrections if needed.	

Name _____.

Spelling Test

Directions: As your teacher reads your words, write each spelling word on the blanks below.

1) _____

2) _____

3) _____

4) _____

5) _____

6) _____

7) _____

8) _____

9) _____

10) _____

Name _____.

Story Map - Animals that Dig

18.5 Reading Worksheet

Pixie's Surprise

Directions: Complete the story map to identify the main characters, setting, and events in the story, "**Pixie's Surprise**". Explain the problems and solutions.

Story Map

The Characters:
(Who)

Title: Pixie's Surprise

The Setting:
(Where)

Events:
(What)

Event 1:

Event 2:

Event 3:

Problem:

Solution:

121

18.5 - Animals That Dig

18.5 Grammar Worksheet

Name _____.

Grammar – *Animals that Dig*

Directions: Is the **bold** word in each sentence a noun, pronoun or verb? Write your answer on the line.

1. I found these **books** in the library. _____

2. You **sing** beautifully! _____

3. Did **she** find out why the show was not on last night? _____

4. I wish we could go to **Florida**. _____

5. How many cookies **did** we **bake**? _____
   _____

*Write a sentence using a **noun**. Circle the noun.*

6. _____
   _____

*Write a sentence using a **pronoun**. Circle the pronoun.*

7. _____
   _____

*Write a sentence using a **verb**. Circle the verb.*

8. _____
   _____

Weekly Sight Words

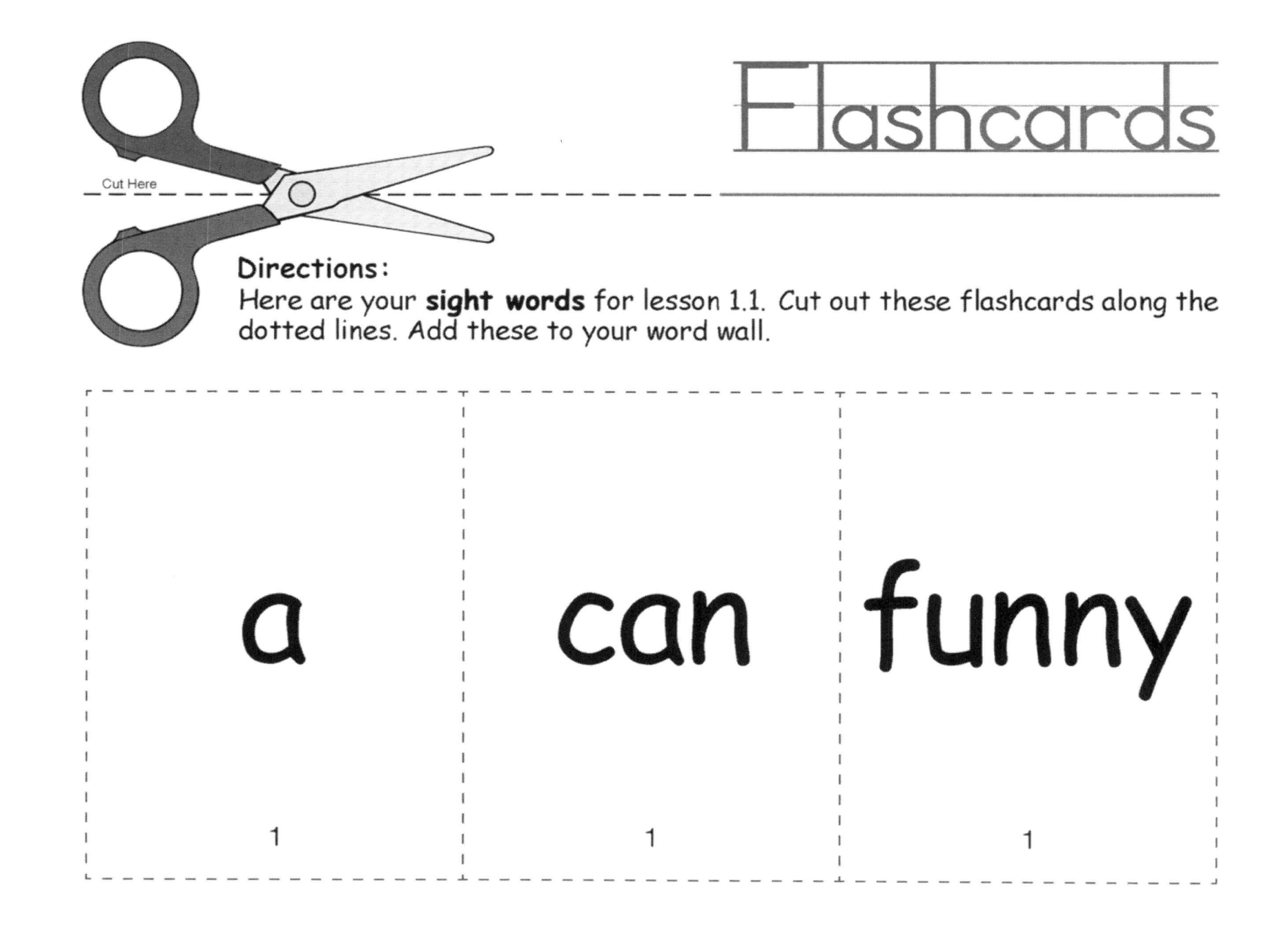

Directions:
Here are your **sight words** for lesson 1.1. Cut out these flashcards along the dotted lines. Add these to your word wall.

Flashcards

a	can	funny
1	1	1

1.1 - Your Family

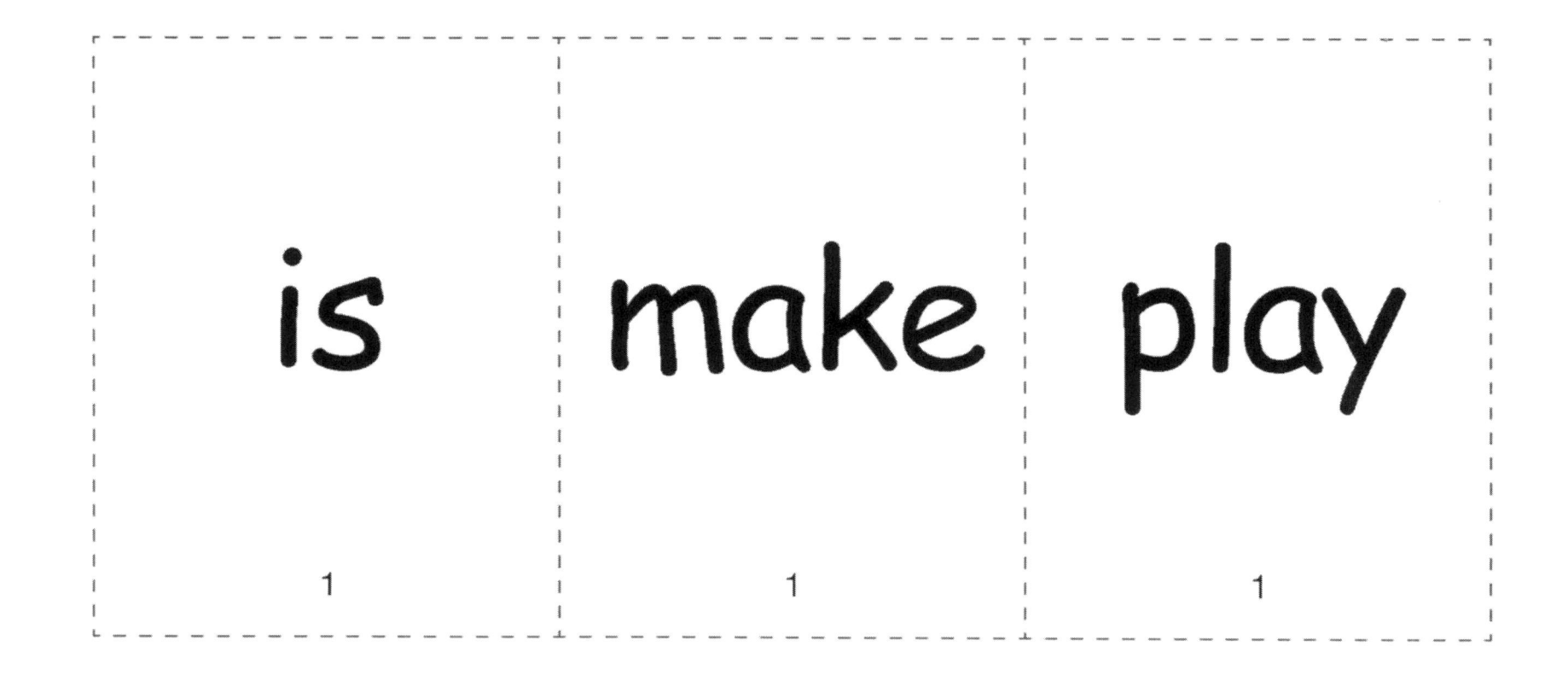

| is | make | play |

the

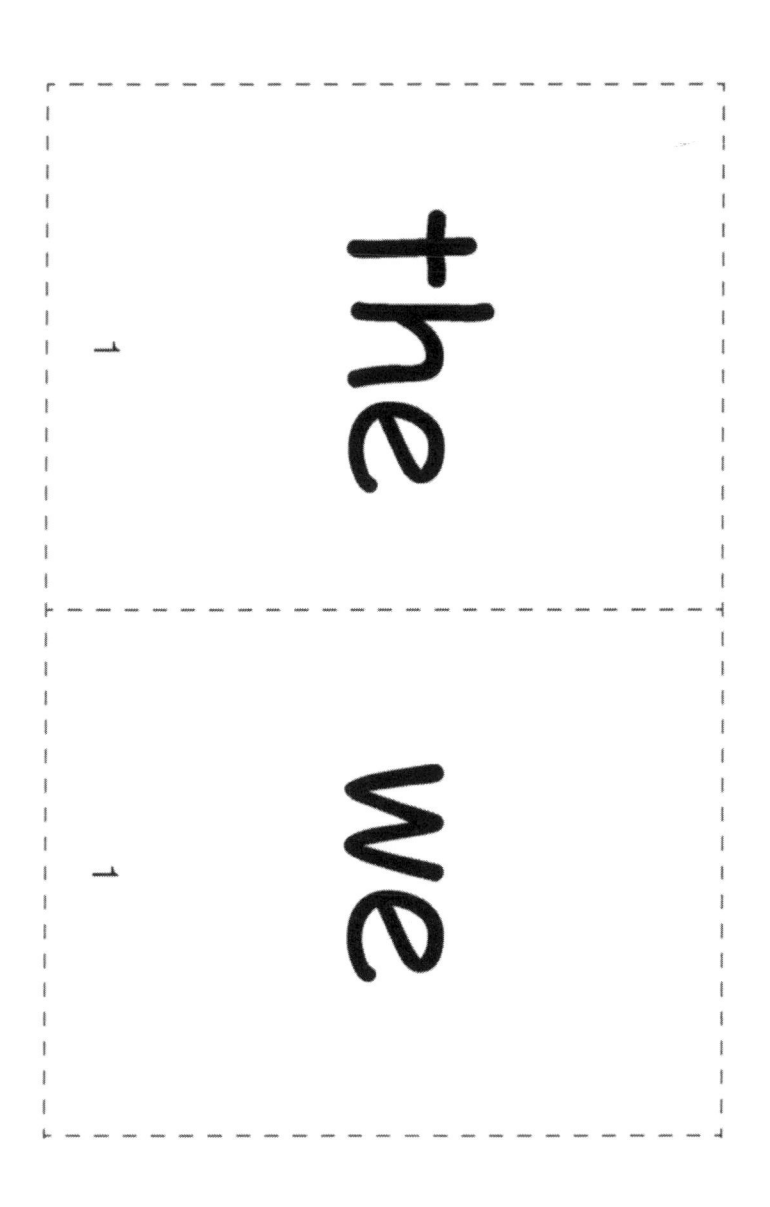

we

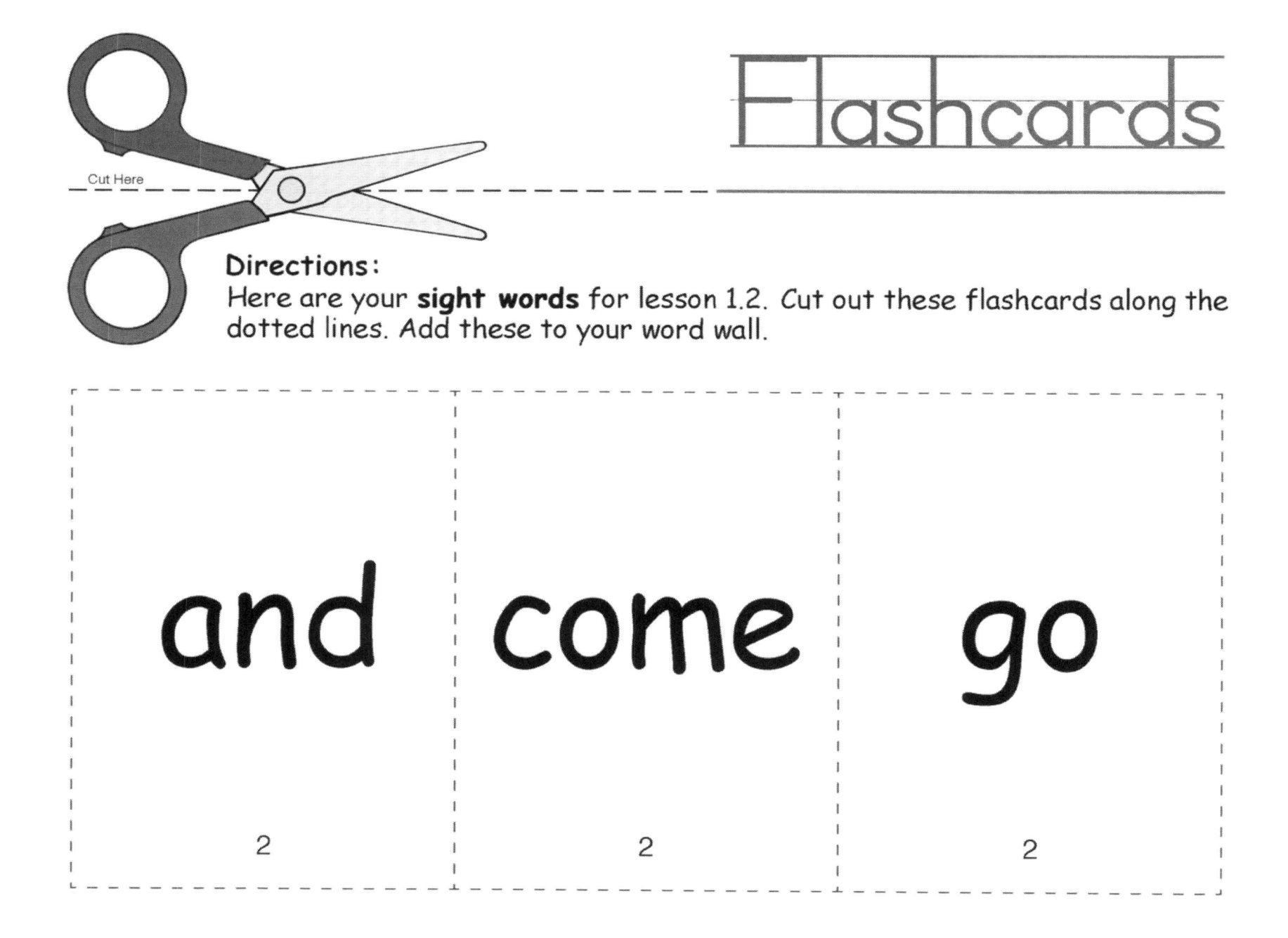

Directions:
Here are your **sight words** for lesson 1.2. Cut out these flashcards along the dotted lines. Add these to your word wall.

Flashcards

| and | come | go |

it

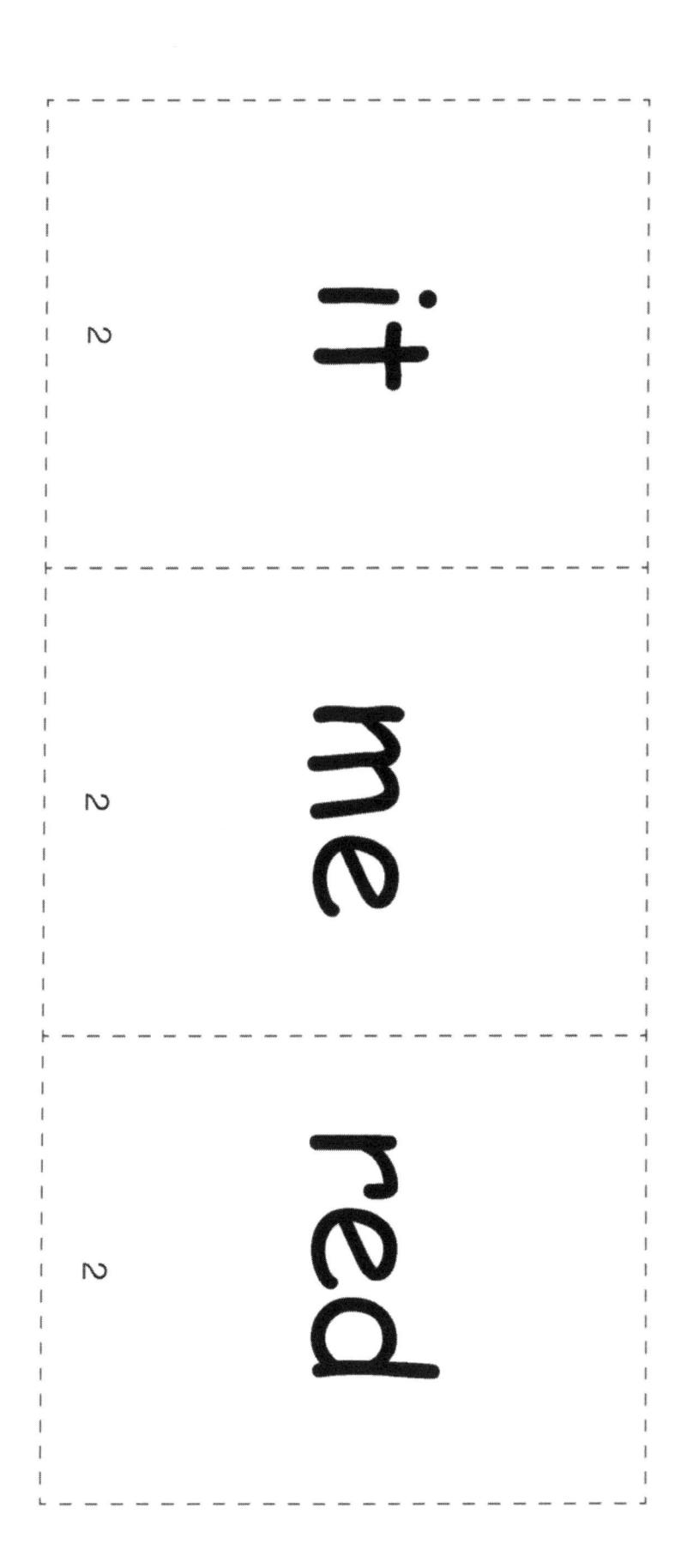

2

me

2

red

2

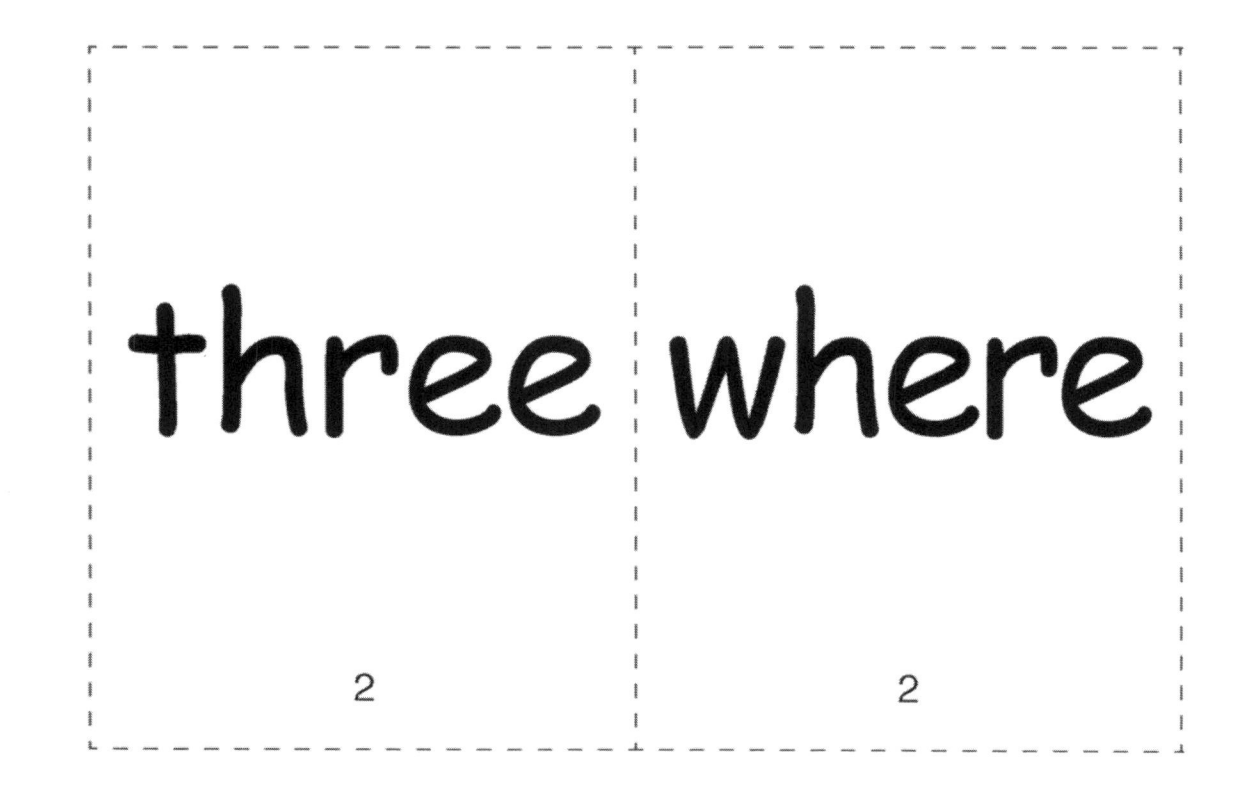

three | 2

where | 2

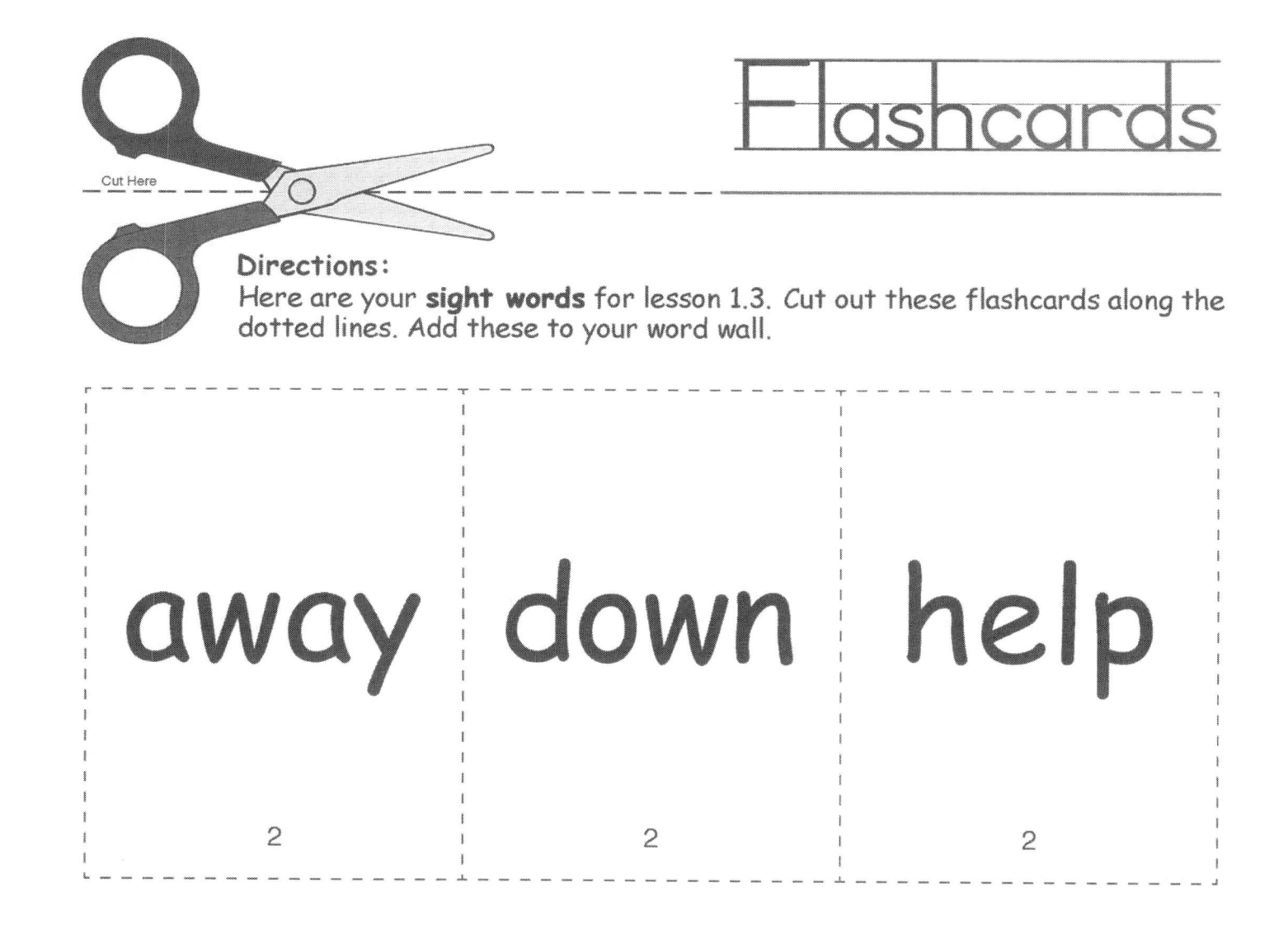

Directions:
Here are your **sight words** for lesson 1.3. Cut out these flashcards along the dotted lines. Add these to your word wall.

Flashcards

away	down	help

1.3 - Your Family

jump	2
my	2
run	2

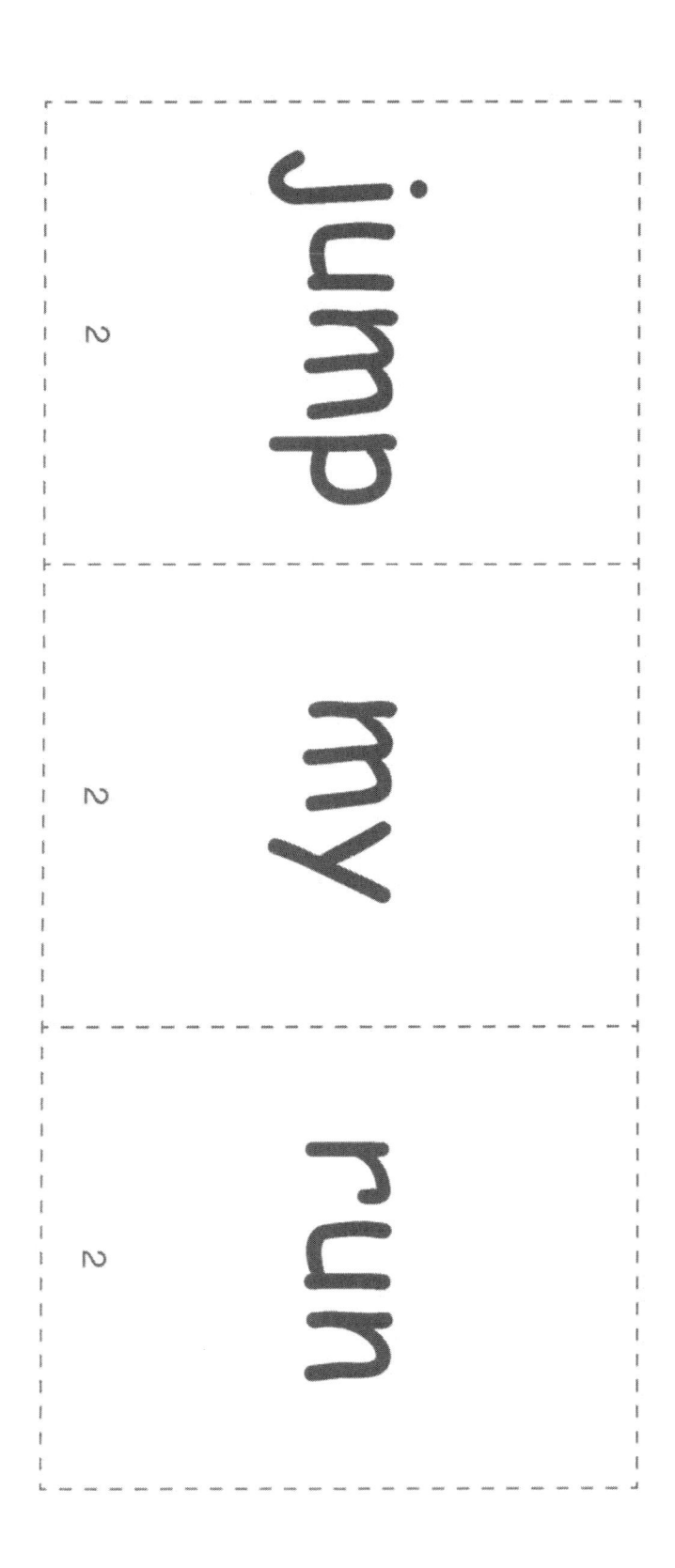

to	2
yellow	2

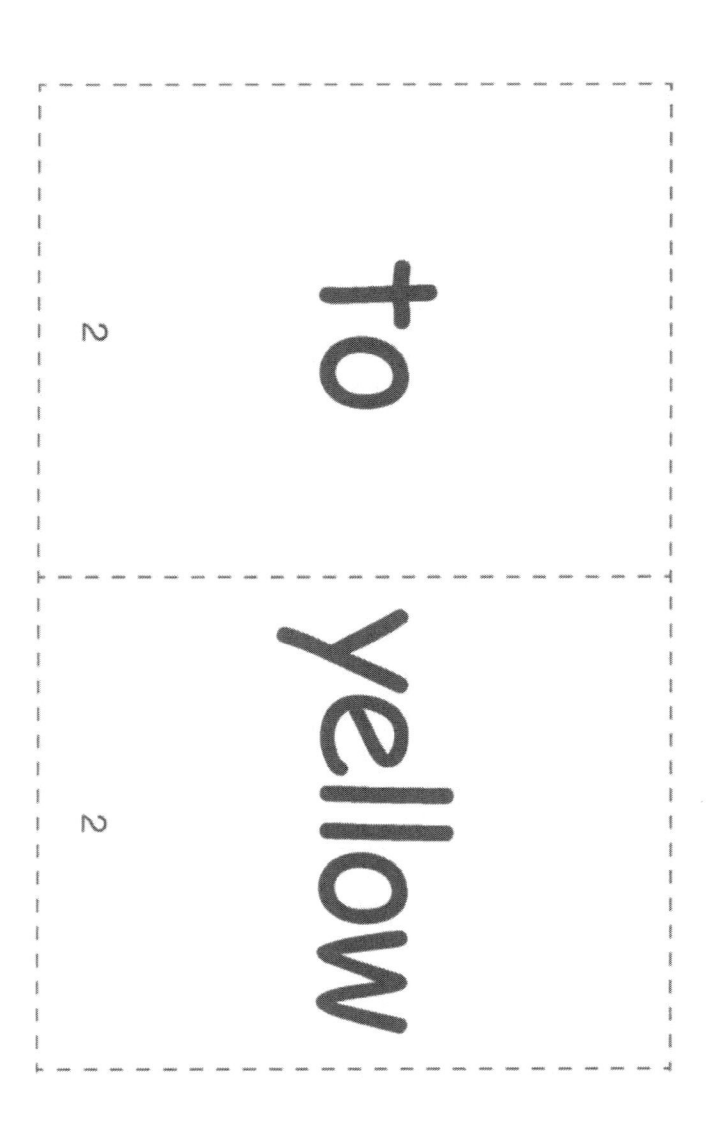

Directions:
Here are your **sight words** for lesson 1.4. Cut out these flashcards along the dotted lines. Add these to your word wall.

Flashcards

| big | find | here |

1.4 - Your Family

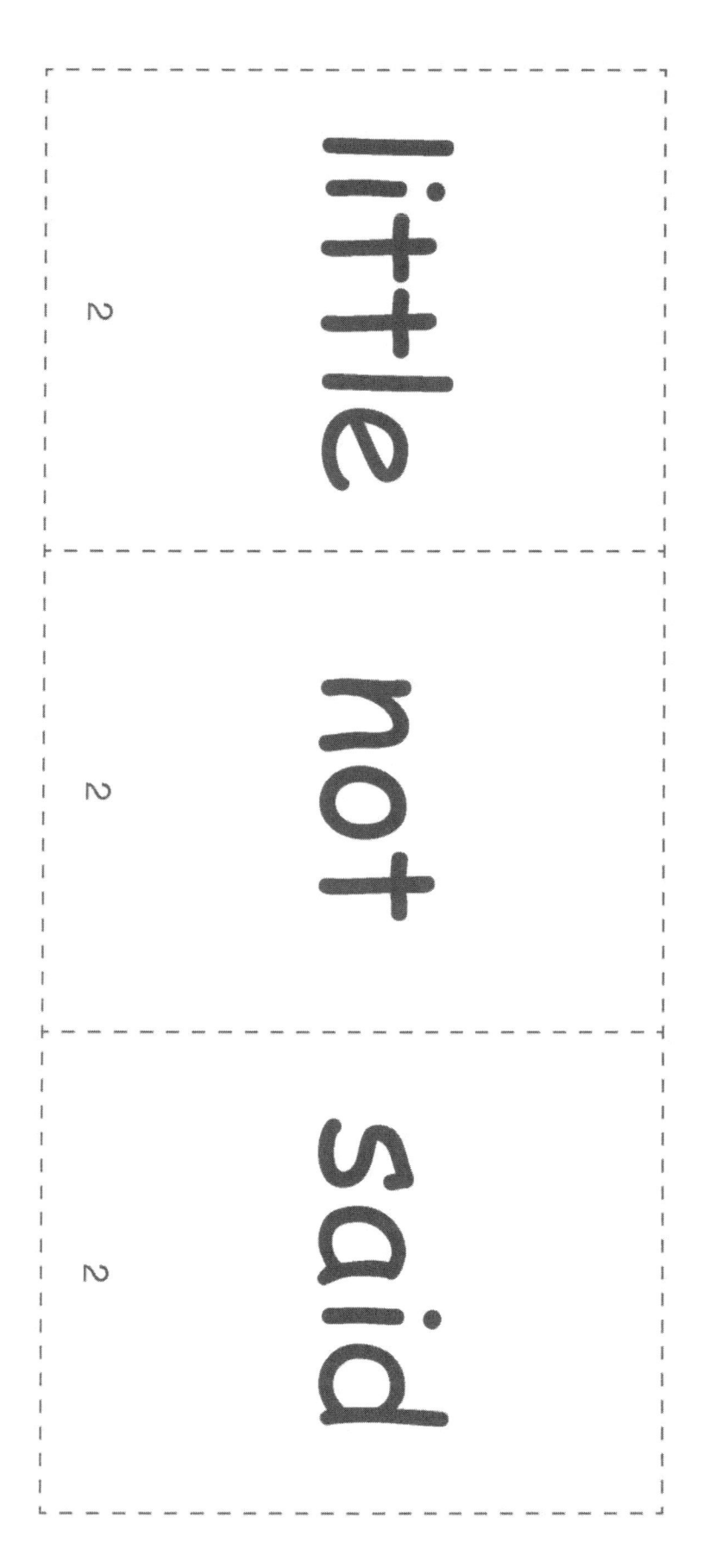

1.4 - Your Family

little	2
not	2
said	2

two	you
2	2

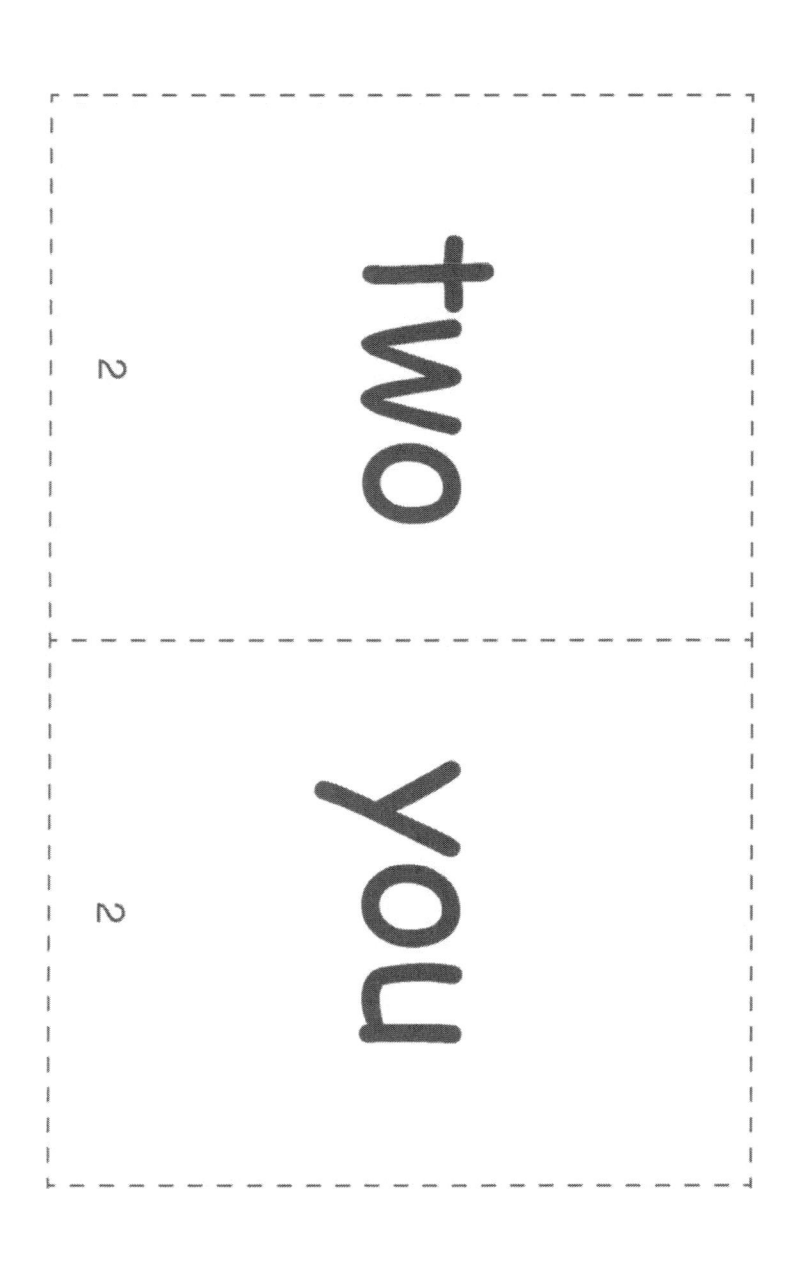

Directions:
Here are your **sight words** for lesson 1.5. Cut out these flashcards along the dotted lines. Add these to your word wall.

Flashcards

blue	for	in
2	2	2

1.5 - Your Family

look	2
one	2
see	2

2

up

Sight Word Cards

Here are your sight words for lesson **2.1**. Cut out these flashcards along the dotted lines. Add these to your word wall.

Family Vacation

Flashcards

all	be	did
good	must	our

Cut them out!

2.1 - Family Fun

ride

soon

Directions:
Here are your **sight words** for lesson 2.2. Cut out these flashcards along the dotted lines. Add these to your word wall.

Flashcards

| too | went | with |

am	black	do
1	1	1

have

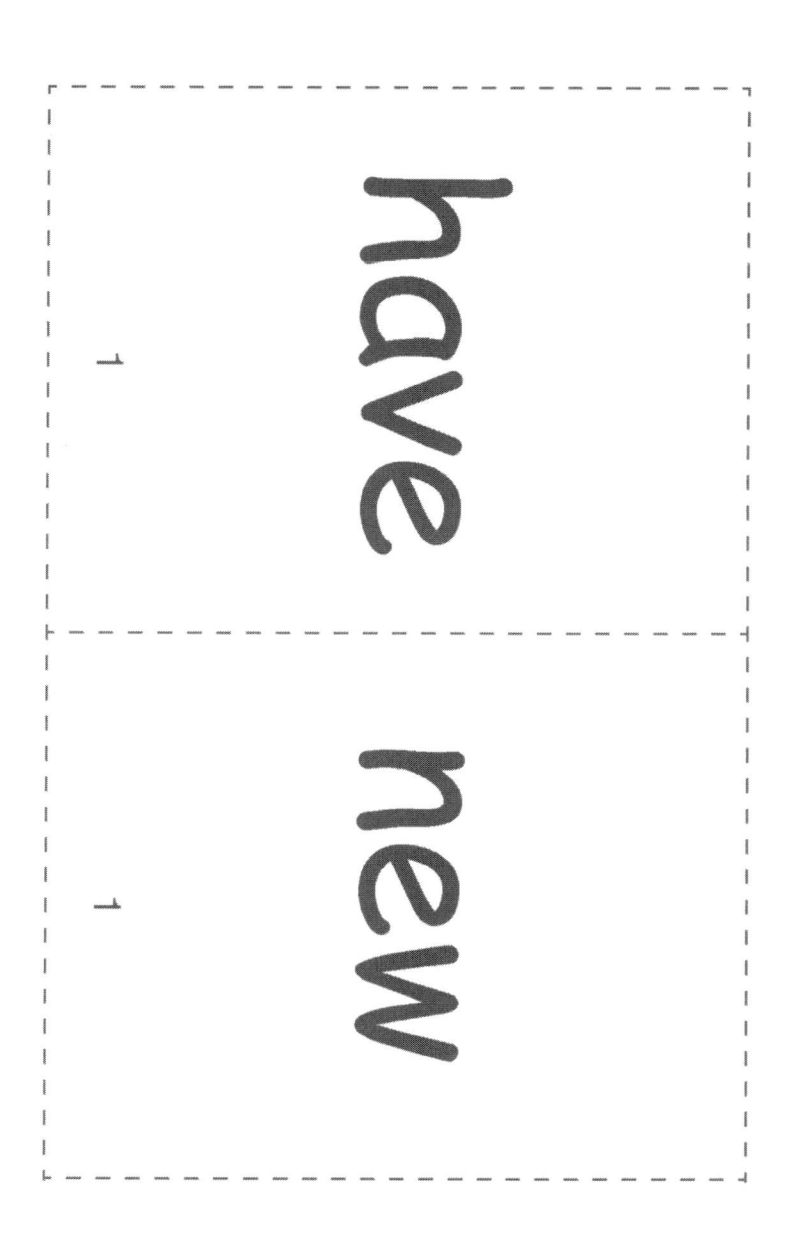

new

Sight Word Cards

Family Vacation

Here are your sight words for lesson **2.3**. Cut out these flashcards along the dotted lines. Add these to your word wall.

Cut them out!

out	saw	that
under	what	yes

Flashcards

are

brown

Family Vacation

Sight Word Cards

Here are your sight words for lesson **2.4**. Cut out these flashcards along the dotted lines. Add these to your word wall.

Cut them out!

Flashcards

eat	he	no
please	say	there

2.4 - Family Fun

want

white

Sight Word Cards

Here are your sight words for the week. Cut out these flashcards along the dotted lines. Add these to your word wall.

Cut them out!

at	but	four
into	now	pretty

Flashcards

3.1 - Bedtime

she

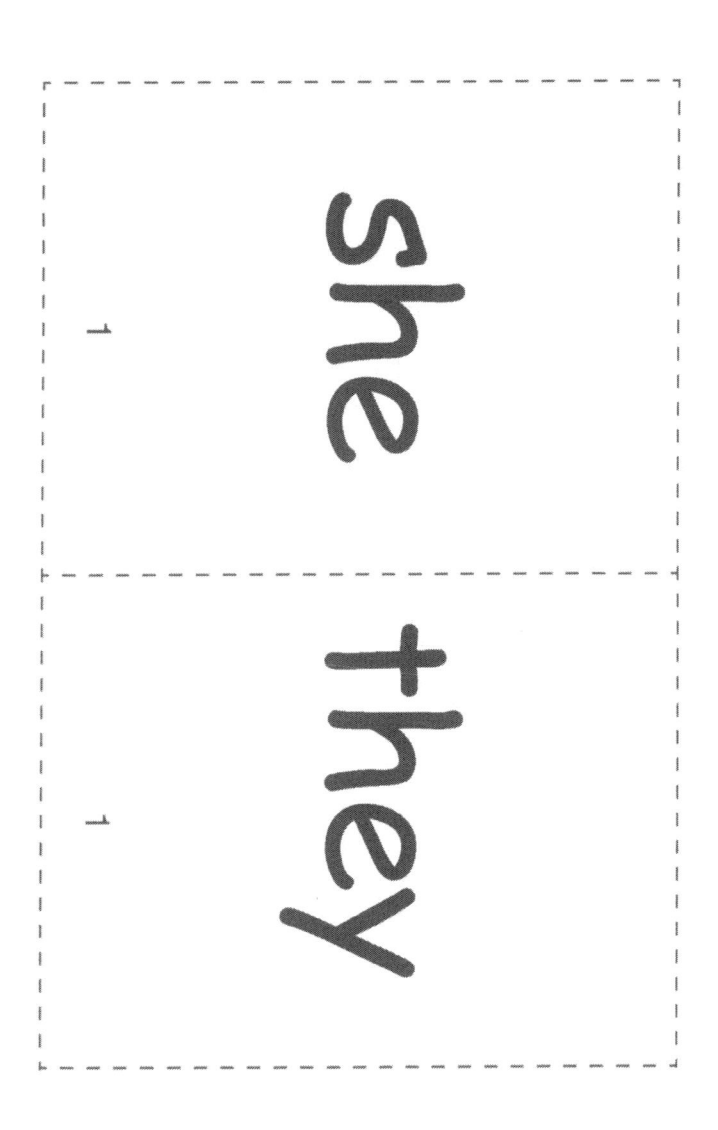

they

Sight Word Cards

Here are your sight words for the week. Cut out these flashcards along the dotted lines. Add these to your word wall.

on	ran	so
this	well	will

Cut them out!

Flashcards

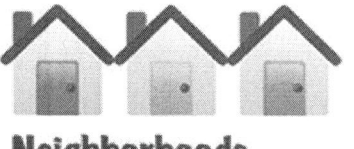

Neighborhoods

Sight Word Cards

Here are your sight words for the week. Cut out these flashcards along the dotted lines. Add these to your word wall.

Cut them out!

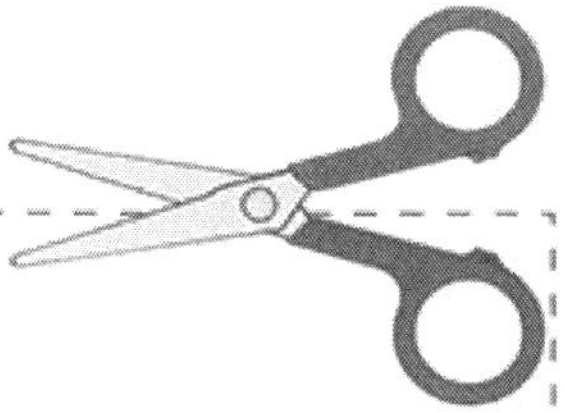

on	ran	so
this	well	will

Flashcards

4.1 - Fall Fun

Neighborhoods

Sight Word Cards

Here are your sight words for the lesson. Cut out these flashcards along the dotted lines. Add these to your word wall.

Cut them out!

Flashcards

after	ask	from
her		

Sight Word Cards

Here are your sight words for the lesson. Cut out these flashcards along the dotted lines. Add these to your word wall.

know	old	round
them	when	again

Cut them out!

Flashcards

5.1 - Farm Visit

Sight Word Cards

Here are your sight words for this lesson. Cut out these flashcards along the dotted lines. Add these to your word wall.

by	give	let
once	same	

Cut them out!

Flashcards

5.3 - Farm Visit

Sight Word Cards

Here are your sight words for this lesson. Cut out these flashcards along the dotted lines. Add these to your word wall.

Dentist Visit

Cut them out!

then	with	an
could	going	his

Flashcards

6.1 - Dentist Visit

Sight Word Cards

Here are your sight words for this lesson. Cut out these flashcards along the dotted lines. Add these to your word wall.

live	open	stop
think		

Cut them out!

6.3 - Dentist Visit

Spelling - *Grandparents*

Sight Word Cards

Here are your sight words for the week. Cut out these flashcards along the dotted lines. Add these to your word wall.

any

has

take

over

Cut them out!

Flashcards

Spelling - *Grandparents*

Sight Word Cards

Here are your sight words for the week. Cut out these flashcards along the dotted lines. Add these to your word wall.

Flashcards

Cut them out!

as

how

thank

were

7.3 - Grandparents

Sight Words - *Making Snow*

Sight Word Cards

Here are your sight words for this lesson. Cut out these flashcards along the dotted lines. Add these to your word wall.

Cut them out!

every	had	may
put	fly	just

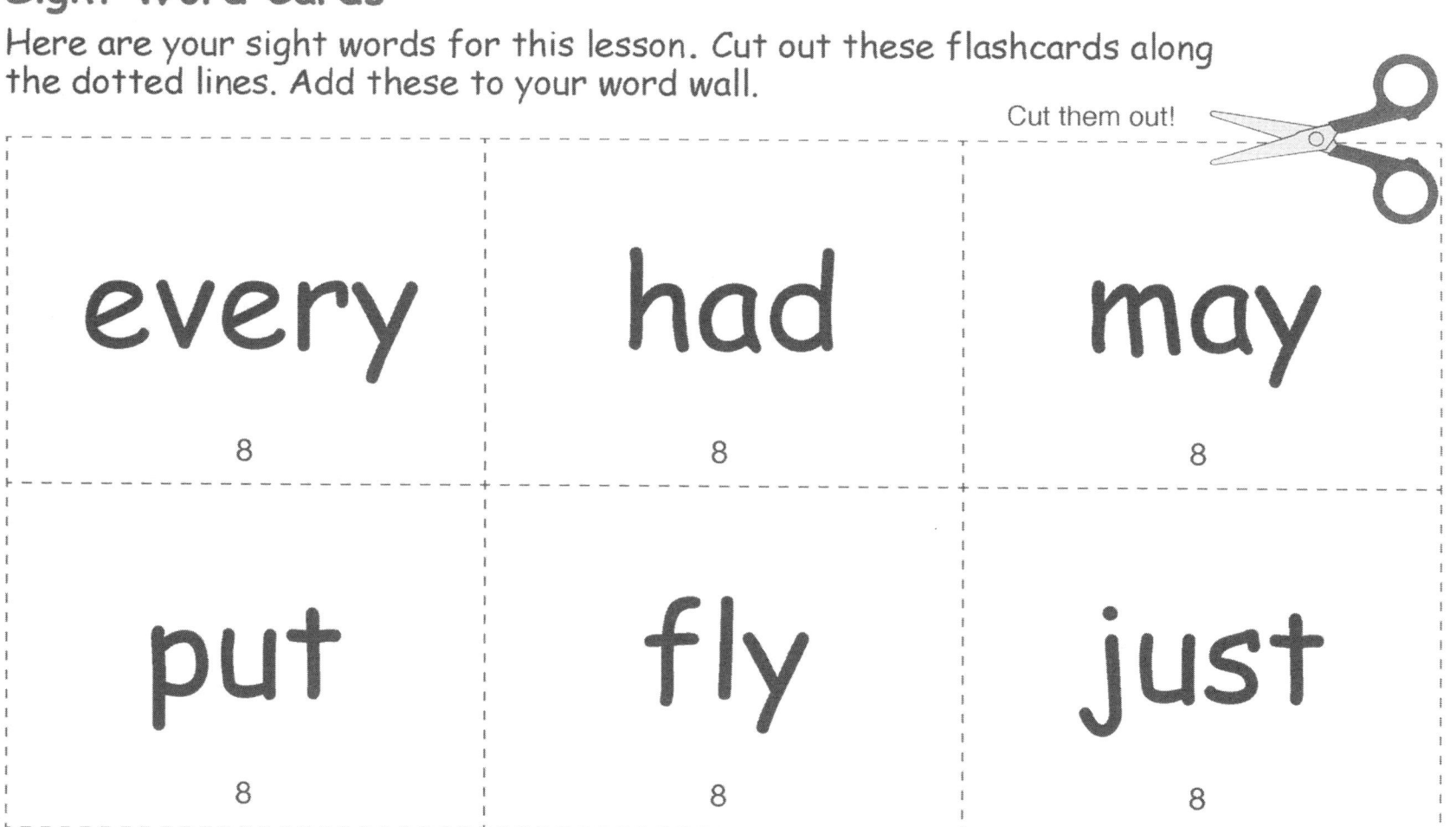

Flashcards

8.1 - Making Snow

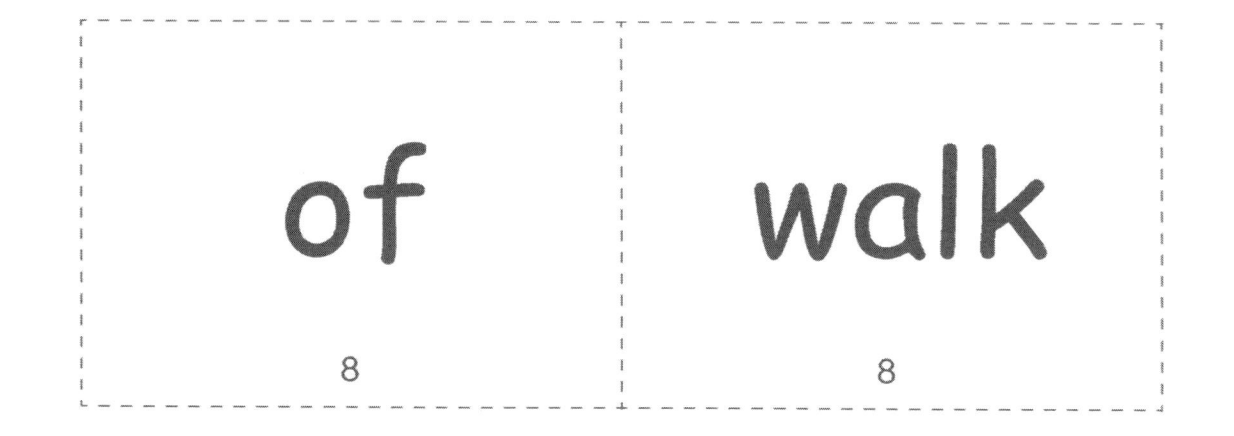

of

walk

Sight Words - *Winter Time*

Sight Word Cards

Here are your sight words for this lesson. Cut out these flashcards along the dotted lines. Add these to your word wall.

always	best	does
found	made	read

Cut them out!

Flashcards

tell	us	why
your		

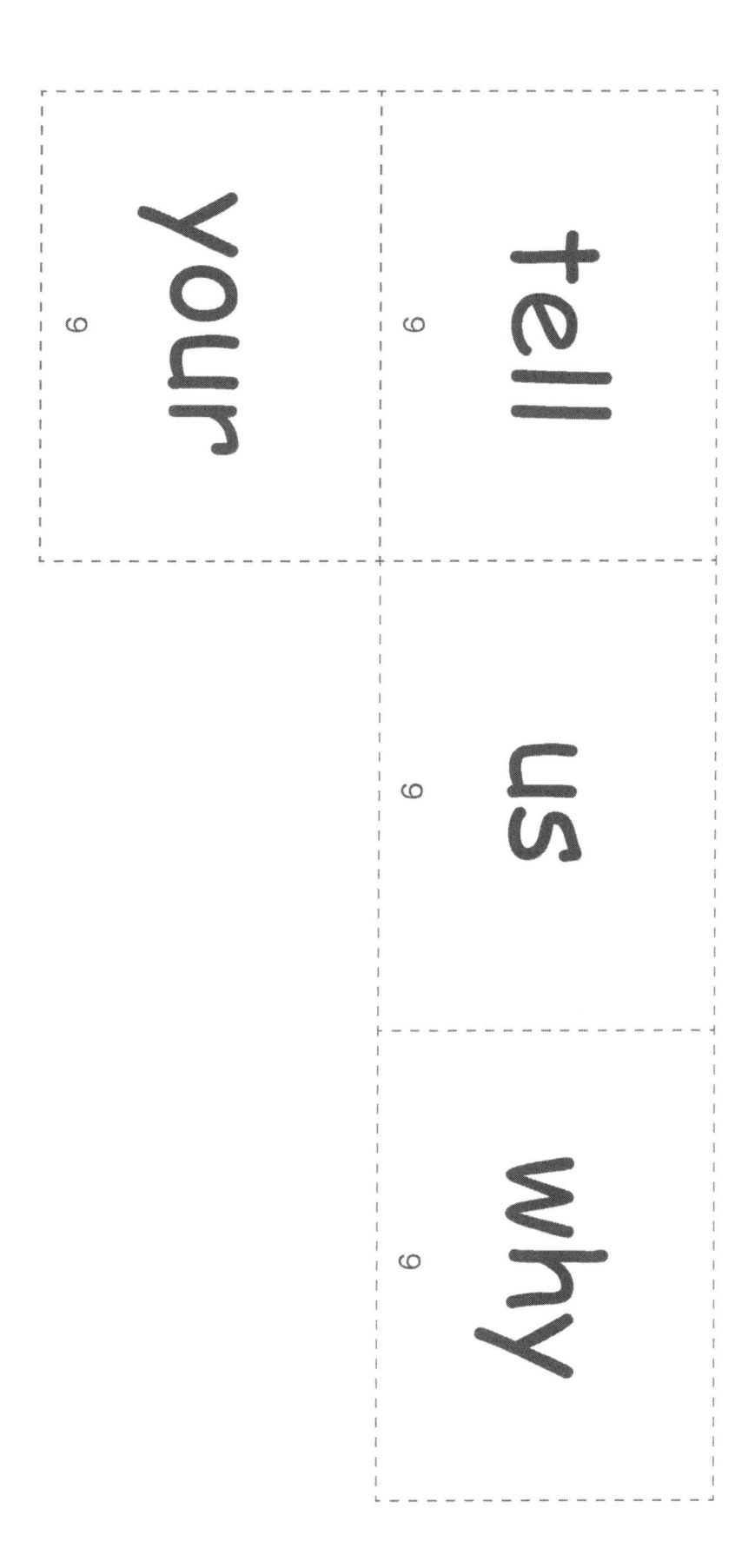

Sight Words - *Cooking Fun*

Sight Word Cards

Here are your sight words for this lesson. Cut out these flashcards along the dotted lines. Add these to your word wall.

Cut them out!

around	both	don't
10	10	10

gave	many	right
10	10	10

Continue on the next page.

10.1 - Cooking Fun

their	10
use	10
wish	10

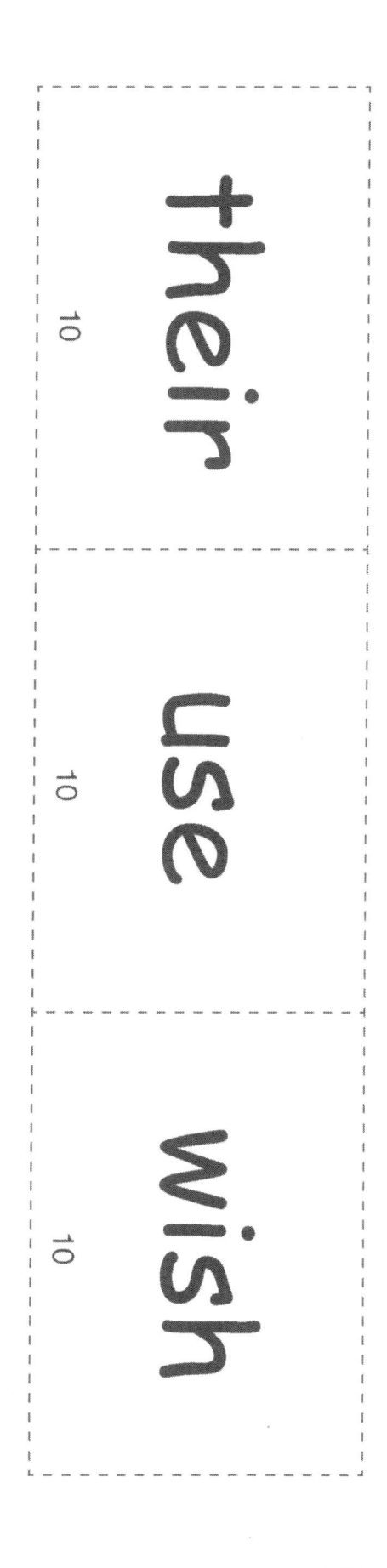

10.1 - Cooking Fun

Sight Words - *Cycles*

Sight Word Cards

Here are your sight words for this lesson. Cut out these flashcards along the dotted lines. Add these to your word wall.

Flashcards

Cut them out!

because	but	fast
goes	off	sing

11.1 - Cycles

these

very

work

Sight Words - *Getting Creative*

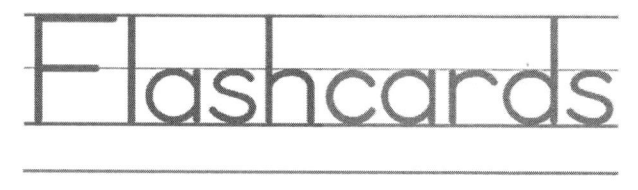

Sight Word Cards

Here are your sight words for this lesson. Cut out these flashcards along the dotted lines. Add these to your word wall.

Cut them out!

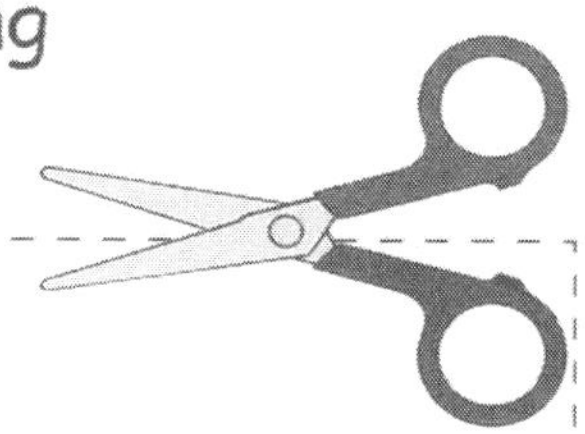

been	call	first
12	12	12
green	or	sit
12	12	12

Flashcards

12.1 - Getting Creative

those	12
wash	12
would	12

Sight Words - *Fun with Friends*

Sight Word Cards

Here are your sight words for this lesson. Cut out these flashcards along the dotted lines. Add these to your word wall.

Cut them out!

Flashcards

before	cold	five
13	13	13
its	pull	sleep
13	13	13

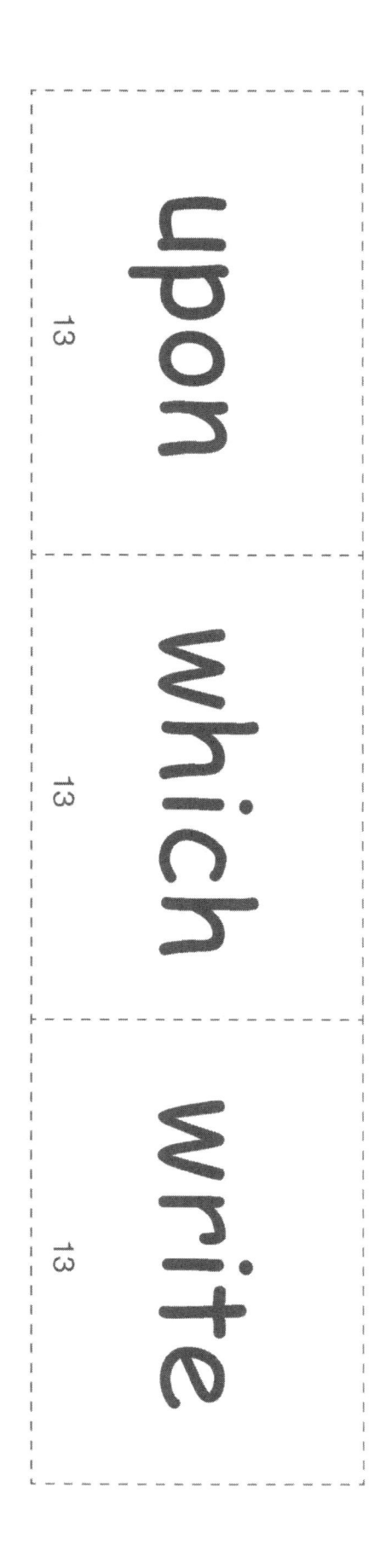

13.1 - Fun with Friends

upon

which

write

Sight Words - *Authors*

Sight Word Cards

Here are your sight words for this lesson. Cut out these flashcards along the dotted lines. Add these to your word wall.

Flashcards

Cut them out!

why	found	because
18	18	18

best	upon	these
18	18	18

18.1 - Animals That Dig

sing

wish

many

Like a Love Song

Nikita Singh is the bestselling author of eight novels, including *After All This Time*, *The Promise* and *Someone Like You*, as well as a contributing author to books in The Backbenchers series. She is the editor of the collections of short stories *25 Strokes of Kindness* and *The Turning Point*.

Nikita was born in Patna and raised in Indore, where she was brought up in a home of voracious readers. After graduating from college, she worked with publishers in Delhi as an editor and publishing manager. In 2013, she received a Live India Young Achievers Award. She is currently an MFA candidate in Creative Writing at The New School in New York City.

You can find her on Twitter, Instagram and Snapchat (@singh_nikita) or on Facebook.

NIKITA SINGH

Like a Love Song

HARLEQUIN INDIA PVT LTD

First published in India in 2016 by Harlequin
An imprint of HarperCollins *Publishers* India

Copyright © Nikita Singh 2016

P-ISBN: 978-93-5177-803-5
E-ISBN: 978-93-5177-804-2

4 6 8 10 9 7 5 3

Nikita Singh asserts the moral right
to be identified as the author of this work.

This is a work of fiction and all characters and incidents described in this book are the product of the author's imagination. Any resemblance to actual persons, living or dead, is entirely coincidental.

All rights reserved. No part of this publication may be reproduced,
stored in a retrieval system, or transmitted, in any form or by any means,
electronic, mechanical, photocopying, recording or otherwise,
without the prior permission of the publishers.

HarperCollins *Publishers*
A-75, Sector 57, Noida, Uttar Pradesh 201301, India
1 London Bridge Street, London, SE1 9GF, United Kingdom
Hazelton Lanes, 55 Avenue Road, Suite 2900, Toronto, Ontario M5R 3L2
and 1995 Markham Road, Scarborough, Ontario M1B 5M8, Canada
25 Ryde Road, Pymble, Sydney, NSW 2073, Australia
195 Broadway, New York, NY 10007, USA

Typeset in 11/14.2 Minion
Saanvi Graphics Noida

Printed and bound at
Thomson Press (India) Ltd

*This is for all the small-town girls,
showing the world how it's done.
#girlpower*